Out of the Skin
Into the Soul

The Art of Aging

DOROTHY ALBRACHT DOHERTY

MARY COLGAN MCNAMARA

San Diego

LuraM

Cover image by Sara Steele.
  "Glory Hole" © 1985 by Sara Steele. All rights reserved.
  Collection of LaSalle University, Philadelphia.
Cover design by Tom Jackson, Philadelphia.

A word about the cover image: A "glory hole" refers to a furnace used in glass-making to soften the glass when it becomes stiff and also to an opening directly into the interior of such a furnace. A person looking from the outside in through a "glory hole" will see the intense fire burning inside the furnace.

A word about the title: "Out of the Skin Into the Soul" is from Pablo Neruda's poem "Death Alone," translated by Angel Flores, from RESIDENCE ON EARTH. *Copyright © 1946 by New Directions. Used by permission of New Directions Publishing Corp.*

LuraMedia
7060 Miramar Road, Suite 104
San Diego, CA 92121

Library of Congress Cataloging-in-Publication Data
Doherty, Dorothy Albracht.
    Out of the skin into the soul : the art of aging / Dorothy Albracht Doherty,
  Mary Colgan McNamara.
        p.   cm.
    Includes bibliographical references.
    ISBN 0-931055-81-4
    1. Aging--Social aspects. 2. Aging--Psychological aspects. 3. Aged--Life
  skills guides. 4. Children's stories. I. McNamara, Mary Colgan. II. Title.
  HQ1061.D57   1993
  305.26--dc20   93-7270
                                                                          CIP

The authors would like especially to thank the publishers and copyright owners of the children's stories upon which this book is based for their permission to quote and adapt their copyrighted material:

From BIMWILI AND THE ZIMWI by Verna Aardema. Copyright © 1985 by Verna
    Aardema. Used by permission of Dial Books for Young Readers, a division of
    Penguin Books USA Inc.
From A HOUSE FOR HERMIT CRAB by Eric Carle. Copyright © 1987 by Eric
    Carle Corp. Used by permission of Picture Book Studio.
From MISS RUMPHIUS by Barbara Cooney. Copyright © 1982 by Barbara Cooney
    Porter. Used by permission of Viking Penguin, a division of Penguin Books USA
    Inc.
From FREDERICK by Leo Lionni. Copyright © 1967 by Leo Lionni. Used by
    permission of Pantheon Books, a division of Random House, Inc.

The authors would also like to thank the following copyright owners for their permission to reprint their copyrighted material:

Quotation from JACOB THE BAKER by Noah benShea. Copyright © 1989 by Noah benShea. Reprinted by permission of Random House, Inc.

Quotation from AGE OF IRON by J.M. Coetzee. Copyright © 1990 by J.M. Coetzee. Reprinted by permission of Random House, Inc.

Quotation from "The New Golden Age of Kids Books" by Michael Dirda, CONNOISSEUR, Sept. 1990. Reprinted by permission.

Quotation from WOMEN WHO RUN WITH THE WOLVES by Clarissa Pinkola Estés, Ph.D. Copyright © 1992 by Clarissa Pinkola Estés, Ph.D. Reprinted by permission of Random House, Inc.

Quotation from "The Golden Girls." Copyright © Touchstone Pictures and Television.

Quotations from "To Grow in Wisdom" from THE INSECURITY OF FREEDOM by Abraham Joshua Heschel. Copyright © 1964, 1966 by Abraham Joshua Heschel. Reprinted by permission of Farrar, Straus & Giroux, Inc.

Quotation from THE SEARCH FOR THE BELOVED by Jean Houston. Copyright © 1987 by Jean Houston. Adapted with permission of The Putnam Publishing Group.

Quotation from "Why Are Americans Afraid of Dragons?" Copyright © by Ursula K. Le Guin; first appeared in PNLA QUARTERLY; reprinted by permission of the author and the author's agent, Virginia Kidd.

Quotation from CROW AND WEASEL by Barry Lopez. Text copyright © 1990 by Barry Holstun Lopez. Published by North Point Press and reprinted by permission of Farrar, Straus & Giroux, Inc.

Quotations from OLD AGE: JOURNEY INTO SIMPLICITY by Helen M. Luke. (New York: Parabola Books, 1987). Copyright © by The Society for the Study of Myth and Tradition. Reprinted by permission of the publishers.

Quotation from "Death Alone" by Pablo Neruda, translated by Angel Flores, from RESIDENCE ON EARTH. Copyright © 1946 by New Directions. Reprinted by permission of New Directions Publishing Corp.

Quotation from W OR THE MEMORY OF CHILDHOOD by Georges Perec. Translated by David Bellos. Copyright © 1988 by David R. Godine and William Collins Sons & Co. Ltd. Reprinted by permission of David R. Godine, Publisher.

Quotation from "A Letter to William Carlos William" by Kenneth Rexroth from THE SIGNATURE OF ALL THINGS. Copyright © 1949 by Kenneth Rexroth. All Rights Reserved. Reprinted by permission of New Directions Publishing Corporation.

Quotation from AS WE ARE NOW by May Sarton. Copyright © 1973 by May Sarton. Reprinted by permission of W. W. Norton & Company, Inc.

Quotation from COLLECTED POEMS, 1930-1973 by May Sarton. Copyright © 1974 by May Sarton. Reprinted by permission of W. W. Norton & Company, Inc.

Quotation from UPANISHADS as it appears in A HOUSE LIKE A LOTUS by Madeleine L'Engle. Copyright © 1984 by Crosswicks Ltd. Reprinted by permission of Farrar, Straus & Giroux, Inc.

Quotation from "Haiku" by Wakuan-Shitai, ZEN POETRY, edited by Lucien Stryk. Copyright © 1972 by Lucien Stryk. Published by Penguin Books USA Inc. Reprinted by permission of Lucien Stryk.

To Dora, Florence, Dorothy,
Thad, Anna, Joseph, Cecilia,
Joseph, Elizabeth, Henry, Rose, Peter . . .
our predecessors in the work

To Dominic and Christian . . .
our life companions in the work

To Sabina . . .
present at this book's conception
and midwife to its birth,
muse, and our sister in the work

To David, Sarah, Christian,
Rachel, Mark, and their children's children . . .
the inheritors of the work

There are lonely cemeteries,
graves full of bones without sound,
the heart passing through a tunnel,
dark, dark, dark,
as in a shipwreck we die from within,
as we drown in the heart,
as we fall out of the skin into the soul.

— Pablo Neruda

Contents

Preface

One bright shining morning almost four years ago, over a round table and Rice Krispies, this book arose out of the union of our personal and professional lives. At that time, we were both reading children's stories to our preschoolers while teaching college courses in literature and psychology to senior citizens. OUT OF THE SKIN INTO THE SOUL represents our response to what is written on aging, most of which we find overbearingly statistical, patronizing, singularly uninspiring — certainly no match for the vibrant, searching, witty, and gracious human beings filling our classes.

Our work with older persons constantly reveals a passion for life not unlike that of the fresh, awe-filled spirit of children. This passion, barely hidden beneath the surface, requires very little kindling to bring the entire life to a glow. One student, Adelaide, when asked why she was attending the personal growth classes, responded, "Well, there are all these ashes in my life, and I figure underneath somewhere there must be some embers."

Stirring the embers of a life ignites a glow akin to the enthusiasm and openness so delightfully manifest in children. The "new" fire comes from the "old" fire born so early in most lives. This fire gathers strength as the life develops. Sometimes it dims, sometimes rages.

The desire to understand life's fire, to search for embers within the ashes of a life, reveals a deep and wise quest for wholeness. OUT OF THE SKIN INTO THE SOUL speaks to this need for inner wholeness. It does so with the most human of all voices — that of story.

Why we use story . . .

Readers of this book may often or on occasion read to young children, as we ourselves do. As we have explored the dimensions and implications of "children's" stories for our own adult lives, it has become increasingly clear what a relatively untapped source of wisdom and insight stories are and how profoundly they link generations when very little else in this culture does. They enliven the child in all of us. Perhaps no one illuminates their beauty and profundity better than Michael Dirda:

> "Children's books, at their exuberant, subversive best, often resemble experimental lit or avant-garde painting more than ordinary fiction. They conjure up, after all, a realm of talking animals and fantastic journeys, where nothing is too bizarre or too wonderful, where wishes come true and there may be a wrinkle in time, a place where one can imagine the impossible three times before breakfast. Nothing alien is alien to it.
>
> " 'For fantasy is true, of course,' says Ursula K. LeGuin . . . . 'It isn't factual, but it is true. Children know that. Adults know it too, and that is precisely why many of them are afraid of fantasy. They know that its truth challenges, even threatens, all that is

false, all that is phony, unnecessary, and trivial in the life they have let themselves be forced into living. They are afraid of dragons, because they are afraid of freedom.' "
("The New Golden Age of Kids' Books," *Connoisseur*, Sept. 1990)

Writing about children's stories challenges us to go in search of these dragons of freedom, to ride on their wings, to be warmed in their fiery breath. We ask each story to release its inner meaning. The stories in this book touch the human heart, as all powerful stories do. But how and why? Because each is a story of the human heart. No matter that the heart's longing be found in the breast of a beast or a hermit crab, that its hope be threatened by robbers or zimwi or mice who lack vision. In the end, against all odds, spirit prevails. Understanding is granted. The taste of wisdom tickles the tongue.

The great gift of stories is their offering of options. In identifying with them, we try out imagined selves, pre-view possible life paths, confront real problems and visualize theretofore unimagined solutions. Why else do children as they listen don costumes, speak in strange tongues and dialects, swagger and swashbuckle, and so create a self that forever beckons them forward?

Through the universality of story, this book is about *us*. We, individually and together, are its central character. Our life experience is its emerging, unfinished plot. It begins with our past and continues far beyond the book cover into our uncharted, yet mysteriously shared future. A future that makes these rich second half years not only formative, as Heschel describes them, but transformative as well:

"May I suggest that . . . potential for change and growth is much greater than we are willing to admit and that old age be regarded not as the age of stagnation but as the age of opportunities for inner growth.

"The years of old age may enable us to attain the high values we failed to sense, the insights we have missed, the wisdom we ignored. They are indeed the formative years, rich in possibilities to unlearn the follies of a lifetime, to see through inbred self-deceptions, to deepen understanding and compassion, to widen the horizon of honesty, to refine the sense of fairness."

(*The Insecurity of Freedom,* p. 78.)

What we mean by "LifeWork" . . .

Inspired by giants like Abraham Joshua Heschel, Helen M. Luke, May Sarton, Henri Nouwen, and Ira Progoff, our search for new models of life integration and transformation, especially in the second half of life, has involved the invention or reclaiming of language that adequately embodies experiences people really have and memories that really drive their lives. After months of considering relatives for the word therapy, we chose the word "eudaemonia": the state of well-being that results from active, rational, spirited, and spirit-filled living.

While therapy sometimes addresses rather narrowly the dysfunctions within a person or group, eudaemonics envisions a more complete human being or community. Strugglers, to be sure. But ever so much more than survivors.

Spirits seized by the *daemon*. Within human life, the daemon embodies the force, passion, genius that carries us forward. The commitment and courage, as it were, to pursue our place of bliss. The small *eu* placed in front of daemon further emphasizes the benevolent face of the spirit, one who accepts darkness as part of the light, one who accepts all levels of dying as part of further life.

The eudaemonic model maintains at the core of its concern the gift of self in all its manifestations: its brokenness and beauty, its wonder and its woundedness. Centers of pain and dysfunction will almost inevitably be touched whenever we work seriously within our lives. Within the eudaemonic model, even the experience of facing past pain aerates the roots of primal power places from which we can draw riches, more expansive energy, neither denying nor minimizing the buried pain.

We call the process of working in a eudaemonic manner "LifeWork," that precious juncture of being and doing wherein all soul has its origin and resting place, its source and growing place. Throughout this book and in our work with people, we offer a eudaemonic model of LifeWork as a vital extension of the therapeutic model of how lives are lived and how people come to the fulness of life.

Such fulness of life can and does come as we enter the later periods of life. Even though society views this largely as a period of decline, it can be a time when devotion to the inner life reveals amazing possibilities.

The energy to discover these possibilities is fired by the re-inhabiting of a life at deeper and richer levels. Acknowledging and loving a life just as it was/is can help us to realize both the wholeness and magnificence of "Who am I."

Each fragment of our lives, then, can become a part of the whole — the blocked, the shattered pieces mending into unity and releasing energy and creativity out of what is already stored in the life. When inner connections are made in this way, we can begin to sense a great at-homeness within both the self and the outer world.

Our basic approach . . .

The movement within this book from story to story is designed to mirror the inner movement of a life from isolated individuality through painful moves and transitions to a deepening sense of community and loving responsibility for the world and its future. At first we projected the book's audience to be senior citizens, possibly seventy and older. Quickly, we saw that people in their fifties found power for their lives in the manuscript. Most recently, it has become clear that the middle thirties is in no way too soon to begin to reflect deeply on the significance of the second half of life.

Each individual chapter also follows a definite pattern: a short synopsis of the children's story on which the chapter is based; a reflective, poetic section to gently tug open the deeper layers of the story; and the text itself. The first appendix provides a suggested LifeWork Exercise for each chapter designed for individual or group use. An annotated bibliography shares some books that have excited and sustained us during different phases of our own journeys.

Approaches you might use . . .

Your journey within this book can be approached in several ways. It is always our hope that you secure a copy of the child's story and read it first for what it will say directly to you, without any mediation. That way your own reflective and imaginative power becomes part of the very process of this book: You coauthor in a deeply creative sense. You can, of course, simply read this book cover to cover. Or you may wish to first enjoy the story synopsis and the poetry at the front of each chapter. If the poetry seems daunting, the text stands on its own and can be read as a book complete in itself. You can use the LifeWork Exercises as you read each chapter or when you complete the entire book. This is a book you "create as you go," as surely as you do your own life.

Whatever method seems best for you, the endpoint of all our reading and journeying is the same — to encourage our passage "out of the skin into the soul," the connatural ground of this season of life, about which May Sarton wrote with such exquisite precision:

"I treasure my soul as something given into my keeping, something that I must keep intact — more, keep in a state of growth and awareness whatever the odds. For whom? For what? That is the mystery. Only when we can conceive of it as belonging to some larger unity, some communion that includes stars and frogs and trees, does it seem valid to 'treasure' it at all. I sometimes feel I am melting into the lovely landscape outside my window. Am floated. For an hour I do nothing else but rest in it. Afterwards I feel nourished. I am one with those gentle old hills." (As We Are Now, p. 19.)

People who inspired us . . .

Each older person whose life we have shared — as student, as friend, as companion traveler — has become for us one of those gentle old hills. In unspeakable gratitude for your nourishment, we have written here what we, supposedly your teachers, have learned from you. You stand at the center of the WE from whom this book received life. Radiating around you in circles of creative energy, we feel other shells of love and encouragement within our lives.

For Mary, these shells include:

Dorothy Gstettenbauer Colgan. Mother and Prime Editor who taught me to love both words and the often wordless wisdom of older people.
Thad Colgan. Father who taught me the sweet shape of the smile within silence.
Kathryn Colgan Herbstrith (1910-1992). Aunt who began a sentence with me at my birth and placed no period to it with her death.
Christine Coulter Henninger (1943-1991). Cousin who lived with a love I can only aspire to. Who dances now where I walk.

The School Sisters of St. Francis. Who offered my life its finest and most lasting models of strength and vision.
Bernice McCarthy. Who in allowing the wheel to discover her has made the world more beautiful for children of all ages.
Dell and John Shadgett. Who believed in this book before there was a book.
The Strull family. Within whose home — during fireworks and after surgery — the first lines of this book were written.
The Thometz family. All of whom in five wonderful ways offer a gathering place for body and spirit.
Rosalyn Lieb. Whose tears at Adam's Bar Mitzvah became words within this book.
Mary Ellen Furstenberg. In whose voice I first heard what we had truly written and was struck with awe.
Becky Atwood. Who responds to my howling every time technology threatens. Musician of Bremen.

✦

Christian. Balancer. Whose being inspires in me the courage to say many necessary "No's," freeing the gift beyond giving, the room of my own. We are becoming human together, a path no other could have walked with me.

Christian Michael McNamara. Who participated with delight in each stage of this book's birth. May you write the book I do not know.

Mark Andrew McNamara. Who first loved the Bremen animals. May you always be my soul's veterinarian.

Punch. Animal familiar who stood sentinel to the spirits throughout the writing.

The millions of innocent, often older women throughout Europe and other places who both lost and gave their lives as witches. At least one of you in her present spirit form breathed this book into being.

✦

Dottie. Dot. Lorene Albracht. Dorothy Albracht Doherty. Who knew and loved me even in my Lazarus disguise and called me forth to life. The rich companionship of whose soul makes it impossible to imagine authoring a book alone. Viaticum.

For Dorothy, these shells include:

Dora Hoelting Albracht (1906-1989). Mother. Death distilled her wisdom and the beauty of her life.

Vincent Ramaekers (1926-1992). Oldest brother. Days before his death called me "Sugar." His loving life stands forever.

Gail Ann Albracht (1936-1991). Sister. Friend. Second mother to our children. Her words were of love, wit, and wisdom.

✦

My brothers and sisters. Who loved me through the grieving process and the writing of this book.

Elaine Sullivan. Sister. Mentor. Guide in my professional development.

The Sisters of St. Benedict. Who provided inspiration, space and time for "soul needs" in my formative years.

The Emeritus Program, Oakton Community College. Who had the foresight to provide classes in personal development to persons over fifty.

Irene and Albert Poll. New and old friends whose loving suggestions improved the manuscript.

Dominic Doherty. Husband. Whose idea it was in the first place that I write down what I was learning. Who was both Mom and Dad to our children and to me during the intense working periods. I am deeply grateful.

David Doherty. Loving son through whose patient coaching I became partially computer literate.

Sarah Elizabeth Doherty. Oldest daughter whose deep identification with Bimwili gave us that story.

Rachel Lorene Doherty. Youngest child who, fresh and full of wonder, delights in story and the story of this book.

✦

Mary Colgan McNamara. Woman. Who joined hands, heart, mind and spirit with mine to create something beautiful for the world. She allowed me to stand on her shoulders and chase out the robbers of self-doubt about writing.

Shells we share include:

Ira Progoff. Who named the underground stream and steeped us in the self-balancing principle within human life.

Abraham Joshua Heschel and Helen M. Luke. Whose profound understanding of the human person at the later stages of life moves us deeply. Heschel has died and Helen, at 88, still graces the earth with her presence in the Michigan woods.

The Brothers Grimm, Eric Carle, Verna Aardema, Leo Lionni, and Barbara Cooney. Whose artful, delightful stories and characters live richly within us.

Judith Duerk. Whose wonderful *Circle of Stones* introduced us to LuraMedia.

Lura Geiger and Marcia Broucek. Who received our manuscript with unimagined grace and transformed it with skill and care.

Sara Steele. Whose cover painting "Glory Hole" crystallizes in a single image the process of using memory for deep LifeWork.

✦

Sabina Agnes Gillespie, O.S.B. Midwife. Mentor. Mystic. Who knows our greatest gift is our heaviest burden. Our words are now yours.

Out of the Skin
Into the Soul

Esteemed readers,
it is a custom in the Orient
to bow as a form of greeting.
Guests do it.
Students bow to teachers to open and close a lesson.
The living bow to the dead
to release them to the world of spirits
so much larger than their own.
This book opens a lesson.
This book begins a journey
to a world of spirits
that are your own.

Two women,
lifelong learners and teachers,
guests in your home,
bow to you.
It is your LifeWork
we have sensed in writing these pages,
its beauty, its pain, its power.
Your courage has called us
past the relentless interruptions
of parenting young children
and working parttime jobs
to help our husbands
feed, clothe, and school them.
This lesson, our shared journey,
invites us out of the skin into the soul.
The youngest among us, at two,
fell in love with Grimms' "The Bremen Town Musicians."
His passion endured hundreds of readings
through dozens of versions
and, unwittingly, freed this book from its block of stone.
Ever since we have walked the road to Bremen.
Let us begin together.

i.

Before Bremen Town

Please! I lived in an old folks' home.
Death visited more often than children.
— "The Golden Girls"

Iron tree blooms,
Cock lays an egg.
Over seventy, I cut
The palanquin ropes.
— Wakuan-Shitai

One parent finds it possible to sustain a dozen children,
yet a dozen children find it impossible to sustain one
parent. . . . Ours is a twin problem: the attitude of society
to the old and aging as well as the attitude of the old to
being old.
— Abraham Joshua Heschel

Four animals, each one rejected by its master because of advanced age and in danger of desertion or death, band together. Donkey, knowing there is something beyond the pasture better than death, decides to leave and make his way to far-off Bremen Town where he hopes to make music. On the way he meets an old, unfed dog, a cat who faces drowning because she can no longer catch mice, and a rooster chosen for the next day's soup. He invites them to go with him to Bremen to make music together. As they bed down for the night in a dark forest, rooster sees a spark of light in the distance. Moving toward the light, they find a hut taken over by robbers whom they must chase out not once but twice. They feast on the robbers' spoils and choose a future in that new home.

THE BREMEN TOWN MUSICIANS
— The Brothers Grimm

The animals start out,
each animal myself,
each master myself,
each robber myself.
Discarded bits,
disowned bits,
disavowed bits of my being.

O donkey self,
how I love you!
Work beast,
you are the broad back
that has carried my burdens to the mill.
Now, even now,
under threat of exile to the pasture,
you, unlikely self, have the vision.
You sense and face the future:
BREMEN. I must go to Bremen.
Donkey, what a lark!
Have you ever been to Bremen?
Do you even know where it is?
How I love your sense of humor,
serious though your journey is.
And all the other selves of me you invite along . . .
motley crew,
troupe of troopers.

My hound dog self,
hang dog,
I love you.
Human's best . . .

therefore, more abandoned.
Not quite the nervy verve of donkey,
but how gladly you go along.
Faithful companion again.

Music? Sure.
That's my best instrument.
I'll support you, donkey.
You lead the way.
I'll heel.

O cat self,
hunter,
for so long you kept my life
from the mouse.
At first you played with it:
cat nip,
cat nap,
kitten prance.
Then stealth became serious
and so did I.
Still, you kept me from the mouse.
Now you want to sit and dream by my fire,
and the master part of me won't allow it.
Somehow you seem more beaten than dog and donkey . . .
Perhaps because you have seen more in your dreams,
heard more in your music,
sweet music of the night?
Slinking, sinking by the roadside,
you see dog and donkey,
receive their invitation —
and dog's promise not to chase.

Musician, you say? Caterwauling?
For shared music, donkey,
may I teach you to dream?

Unlikely trio.
Your sounds need a heart with perfect pitch.
(Teach my heart!)

Across the afternoon
to your perfect hearts
comes the sound,
a morning sound.
You know your time is out of joint.
O blessed spite!
You are even now being born to set it right.

O rooster-out-of-soup,
how about you?

I am crowing all my crows,
could never have guessed there were so many left in me.
The farmer's wife has company.
Will I join yours? you ask.
Bad company for good, I say.

O rooster self,
prideful puff,
I love you with warm laughter.
You stand on the fenceposts of my life.
Gatekeeper.
Spontaneous sentinel of the sun.

How I have looked forward
to your punctuation of my days!
Flop-fly now to your friends and set out,
leaving me to deal with your masters:
miller, huntsman, cottage keeper, cook.

Each master myself —
ME, your master.
Do I now sentence you to die,
lovely company of animal selves?
How far I have fled from my center
to cast you out.
Have I come to believe that old is ugly?

O master self,
I call you back to my center.
How unloved and unlovely you must be feeling
to send out my other selves.
Now you are here with me.
I sense your care, your loyalty,
how much you have done for me all these years,
your weariness,
your fear: Will you, too, be rejected
now that you are tired and old?
O master self,
I thank you. I love you.
I will never cast you out.
I call you to grow as all my selves are growing,
going deeper into this forest night,
seeking shelter on the road to Bremen.

Donkey,
gentle leader,
you say we should stay the night?

The animals settle with a sigh.
Bremen tomorrow,
rest tonight.
On forest floor and branches,
safe spot in the dark.

Rooster,
watchful gyre,
beacon to this night's darkhouse,
seer of sparks,
are we to believe what you see,
what we cannot see? —
A spark in the dark,
a place of light.

Bonded and trusting,
the animals set out once again,
this time across the forest floor
through the endangering darkness.
As they go,
the spot of light grows large.

How are you here, O light?
Is darkness your place of highest glowing?
Who can create such midnight shining?

A hut among the shadowed trees.
Only donkey large enough to look within.

What is it you see?

A feast.
Food enough for us to forget hunger.
A fire for our dreams.
Warm rest.

O donkey,
you who drew us here,
is this our Bremen place?

Rush of breath.
Intake of air.
Impossible to believe:
There are robbers here,
fiends at the feast.
Then a plan:
On each other's shoulders
the four shall become as one,
shall cast a monstrous shadow
on the robbers' wall.
So it is that their music can begin.
Chorus of cacophony.
The bray. The bark. The meow. The crow.
Night music no robber can receive.

O robber self,
you flee.
And I know you must go,
as my animal selves have already gone,
more deeply into this numinous night

to learn what you must know:
A false feast can never fill.
Allow yourself to be cast out,
expelled at last past emptiness,
out finally through fear,
beyond fear.

Yes, we will cast out the robber selves.
Yes, we will feast and stay.
All of us together in a single self —
can a fairy tale ever be so true?
We who now sit at this table,
sleep upon this straw,
we who still breathe Bremen
in our dreams.

✦

I enfold you, O beautiful beasts,
donkey, dog, cat, and rooster,
as together we journey
out of the skin into the soul.

In the wonder-touched world of "The Bremen Town Musicians," children easily fall in love with the warty, saber-toothed robbers and the fact that four lowly animals outsmart them. And what an ingenious victory! Certainly its total intrigue — complete with shadows and imaginary monsters — seems reserved to the very young.

Yet readers who ache with the animals' age likewise applaud the "underdogs," the triumph of the "good guys" over the unseemly forces of avarice and greed, gluttony, robbery, and sloth. This is the victory that readers of any age instantly see and share. It is there, palpable, spine-tingly, clear-cut. The literal level of the story. Yet there is a world of deeper riches, multiple levels of meaning, waiting to be discovered by both young and old who, if fortunate, might find themselves reading "The Bremen Town Musicians" together.

A certain man owned a donkey who bore the grain sacks to the mill without complaint many long years. . . . So begins one of the most enduring of what Jakob and Wilhelm Grimm called their *Household Tales.*

A certain man . . .

How soft-spoken the language of fairy tale, of story, delicately begging entry into our lives. A certain man, not an uncertain one. Who could it be?

The moment that question slips into the mind of the reader, young or old, an intimate identification begins, a shared journey. What is it like to have a donkey? How do heavy grain sacks feel? What will happen when the donkey gets old and tired?

Almost two hundred years after the creation of this story, we still recognize that man, his donkey, and the world as it was before Bremen became the donkey's dream:

A world where four animals had outlived their usefulness, were nearing the end of their "productive" lives.

A world unable to visualize a future beyond work and physical capacity.

A world where the old had no honored place. In truth, no place at all. Only a pasture where each straw of hay or extra bone would be begrudged . . . or the bottom of a well . . . or a kettle of soup . . .

And into that world walks a donkey. Strange visionary! Incongruent dreamer! The plodding one who longs to sing. Who has hidden music within all these long years. How many times on the dusty path to the mill must that donkey have longed for the road to Bremen. A longing that would not go away. Was it spoken of in youth and laughed into silence? Perhaps.

You, a musician? Why, you were born to carry corn. Why else would you have those four strong legs and broad back? Certainly our bodies tell us who we are. Yours should bray, not sing.

Untiringly for many years, the donkey carried the grain sacks to the mill. The broad back refused to be bowed. But two other processes were at work, more hidden, no less true. One was the *fact* of aging. Physical strength was *going:*

Donkey felt more and more unfit to work. The other was the *truth* of inner awakening. Spiritual strength was *growing*: Donkey could see more and more deeply the harm that might come from staying in the master's pasture, from accepting biology as destiny, from surrendering control over personal creativity and personal future.

Donkey knew the time. Time to run away. Transition time. Time to make a break. Time to create a future. The ancient dream of music, so long stilled, arose. The untrod path to Bremen beckoned. *There I will without fail be a town musician.*

Who of us, as we age, can fail to put on donkey hooves, flick a fly with donkey's tail, feel a song within donkey's bray? With donkey — *within* donkey — then, we can go to Bremen.

For us, as for donkey, the road to Bremen is a journey to reclaim the human heart, the deepest self. "The Bremen Town Musicians" rightly focuses this journey in the second half of life when interior and exterior forces often align against such reclamation, when inner music may seem far away or nonexistent, when the world within may feel overshadowed or squelched by societal rejection or personal exhaustion.

What resources have we to bring us to this rich and risky road with donkey? We may feel utterly helpless, may want someone else to drop the meaning of life into our laps. The awareness of the need to gather all our parts, to be whole and holy, escapes so many of us. Society is rife with enticements on the one hand and discouragements on the other, lotions and potions to distort the aging process and thereby deprive us of its meaning.

And we ourselves may grow fearful, believing that we lack the energy, the knowledge, and the personal power to do the work of the second half of life. More than anything else, we need to connect with our personal resources — even if forgotten, disregarded, or poorly nurtured for much of our lifetime.

The journey to Bremen *is* the journey of the second half of life — linking with others, confronting masters who usurp power, routing robbers — every child's fairy tale dream come true! During the first half of life, we gather and gather. We begin with the miracle of our conception, and each day, each moment, from then on allows our story to develop, be it filled with drama, comedy, or be it fairly humdrum.

It is during the first half that we live our childhood, receive the bulk of our education, leave home, form adult relationships, and become productive members of society. Even though we go on to have new experiences and form new relationships, for the most part the significant decisions and events of the first half of life contain the seeds of new life wherever in our lives we may be.

In the second half of life, we deeply reenter our entire life span and learn what we missed in the first half, recognizing the meanings from the first half. Our lives can become rich and profound.

Perhaps in considering this reentry, we feel old and tired, tired out. Our bodies in some cases have broken; our senses may or may not be as keen. Yet we do have our bodies, our donkey selves, that have been with us since the beginning and have gone along for the most part willingly as we grew from childhood.

As we age, the body and the care of the body may begin to take enormous amounts of time, energy, and money. There may be the sense of being put out to pasture or the fear of impending illness, pain, and/or disability. That fear can be enormous, can sap our energy. And still the determination of our donkey self, that beast of burden, serves us, works for us.

Society's view of us as we age can affect and reflect how we see ourselves. The attitude toward growing old, toward aging, is largely negative in Western society. The prospects of being sent to pasture, or *feeling* sent to pasture, are very real. Encouraged by our environment to see ourselves this way, we may mistakenly believe that we must settle for much less than we had hoped. Or perhaps we have no hope at all. Such despair feeds on a fear that we will never reach a place of light or that there is no such place anyway or that we are too tired to look for it.

Against all odds and adversaries, we can lean on the donkey self. That dear donkey self is with us until our last breath is taken. It clings to life with every fiber until it lets go in death. It finds our other selves along the roadside and invites them along on its journey. Because of its basic outgoing, warm nature, it does not threaten the other animals on the way but sustains them in the lessons they have to teach us.

Donkey starts out. Inner clarity and urgency lead away from the harming pastures, the killing fields. For donkey there is no fear of going alone. And even as the journey begins, it is more *toward* than *away from*. What may have started in donkey's heart as an escape from harm — an escape from stagnation, despair, or death — is quickly transformed into creative and creating choice.

Donkey has already walked some distance in solitude, consolidating the future's promise with each forward step, when dog appears. Dog, whose master seeks to kill him since he can no longer hunt. A most important juncture for donkey, the subtle shift from I to WE. There is no thought of exclusion, no thought that Bremen may be big enough for only one musician. Rather, donkey's entire being orients toward inclusion. *What ho, big fellow, why are you panting so?*

Clearly, dog has not yet evolved to donkey's level of awareness. They share advancing age, physical exhaustion, and masters chary of continuing to feed them in their diminished condition. Dog, however, merely asks a question of the unseen future: *Now how will I earn my keep? I want to live, to continue being nourished. I do not expect to be fed without effort. I will do my part. But what part can I have?*

Dog needs donkey's dream. And donkey overflowingly offers it. The nature of a dream: to spill over, to extend itself, to embrace. To translate from the dark consciousness what one spirit hears but many can understand. To form and re-form community. Donkey offers: *I am on my way. . . . Come too.* Dog accepts. The band of musicians, the bond of musicians, begins.

And so, in the simple way of story, dog becomes donkey's first companion. Just as donkey has meaning for the self, so does dog. The dog self is that part of us that lets us know from time to time about being *faithful to ourselves.* Over the years, this self is truly our best friend since it involves unrelenting commitment to be — to *be* in the fullest sense of that word. Sometimes this very faithfulness seems like plodding, like the old dog who never leaves the master. But in the second half of life, there is an urgency about being faithful to the self.

In the earlier years there was so much coming at us — growing up, going to school, perhaps having a family, a job — that we probably were often tired and overwhelmed, with little time to become aware of the plodding. "Pushed along" may have been more accurate. Yet, even then, our dog self was doing the best under the circumstances.

When much of the outside pushing subsides, our faithfulness to ourselves comes to the fore. Not demanding, just looking up into our faces, into our very souls, like the old dog saying — maybe even begging — "Be faithful to yourself." That self has always been there, but it is harder to avoid as we age.

Again society pulls us away, tantalizes with games, retirement homes, get-aways, fun-in-the-golden-years-sun. Such a society can deprive us of this time's deepest fulfillment by taking us away from, rather than toward, our life's center. The struggle to be faithful to the self involves firm and fierce resistance to such centrifugal enticements. There are often long hours alone, maybe lonely hours. There are days and winter days when we may be inside with only the phone to connect us to another. Those are hard times, and sometimes we feel overwhelmed in a way different from when we were younger. Is this all there is? Faithfulness to ourselves becomes of the utmost importance. Self *is* the place where we can learn to find comfort and the meaning of life. That faithful dog self leads us to meaning. We do stand alone. At last we let go of proving ourselves to others and rest in the truth of "who I am."

Unlike the donkey self's physical work, which gradually eases up, our dog self stays and stays. That self is always there even when we do not pay attention to it. So we can call upon this part of us at any time. It will be sitting at the door to our souls.

The visionary donkey offers; the faithful dog accepts. United more deeply than ever, they go on. Before long they see a cat sitting in the road with a face as glum as three days of rain.

Old whiskered one, why so sad?

Familiar response: *My teeth are ground to stumps. I no longer wish to hunt. My mistress wants to drown me for sitting by the fire to sleep.*

Donkey hears the surface words, but hears even more resoundingly cat's hidden being. Once more the invitation is extended: *You are at home with night music, so our life in Bremen is definitely for you.* Of course. Never a doubt. One who understands night music has all that is necessary, an abundance of what their future requires.

For night music is the song of the unconscious, that web of patterns and connections woven in the rich underground world of evolution and history, the collective memory of non-living as well as living beings, that mite of matter through which all of creation shares spirit. Night music melts the separateness of subjectivity and prepares the soul for deep communion.

Once again donkey's vision pierces through to the heart of being. Just as that vision orients the animals to the future, so the kind of dreaming symbolized by cat's night music links them to the flow of the past and to the place of the unconscious in creating that future.

What a task for cat! Yet cat loves the cat work, can never get enough of it: The cat self throughout our lives always invites us to night music.

Ah, the dreams we have for ourselves! That is where the cat self begins, gently drawing us to deeper and wider dreams, planetary plans. Like each animal self, the cat's role changes over a lifetime. In our very young life we dream so freely; we imagine ourselves in all sorts of ways, any way we wish. That free child within, unless beaten down very early, easily imagines.

During the busy young adult and adult years, that dreamy side of ourselves so often gets pushed aside in favor of making a living and being, of necessity, practical. The cat self has little time to wonder, to dream. There is time and space with the gift of aging to do just that, even though many pressing considerations often have to be dealt with in the second half of life: health, housing, losses that seem insurmountable — and are for some.

Time, though, is the gift most present. What to *do* with time. Cat has no problem! As long as she is fed or catches the mice, most any warm spot will do, and the dreaming begins. These dreams are not of mountains to climb nor empires to build. The dreaming is not worrisome: if only I had or hadn't . . . why didn't I . . . what if. . . . Rather, this dreaming is all about that *place*, that *me* still filled with possibilities, still hidden within the deep womb of night music, that me viscerally aware of these older years as my formative ones.

The dreamer wishes for, hopes for, sees visions of possibilities; intuits connections between personal and transpersonal being. The dreamer-within is the part of us free to wonder, to express delight. Like our donkey and dog selves, our cat self, the inner dreamer, is always available. However, it needs time and space to feel inspiration and desire.

Even with the time and space we have always yearned for, the dreamer in us could easily give way to despair. Society may tell us: You're done. You've lived your life. You're not producing, so what good are you except to make money off of — via retirement plans and conspicuous consumption to make your age inconspicuous?

Such a society, a pre-Bremen world, resents aging, fears death, fears nothing more than night music. The cat. The moon. The broom. The lunge toward lunacy. Surrender of *rational* control over self, over life, over the future. Not every society has believed this. Recall one that said, "Your old men [women] shall dream dreams. . . ." (Joel 3:1). And as we become older, we are free — more powerfully than ever before — to create such a society, to devote time and energy to dreams for ourselves and our universe.

Then our dreams arise from long life lived, sometimes in great pain and sorrow, sometimes in joy, enthusiasm, and elation. We definitely have enough memory and life experience to dream of the fulness of life. Years of night music, however dimly heard, are creating the most powerful dreams of which the human heart is capable. We can think of those dreams as fulfilling the self, as fulfillment for our world, our universe. All dreams blended at last to a single dream to which night music has led us.

Yet the sorrowing cat by the side of Bremen's road hears precious little music as donkey and dog approach, sees rather visions of a watery death: *My mistress plans to drown me.* The history of the cat's relationship with humans offers clear evidence of ambiguous and alternating acceptance and rejection. Even semi-domesticated, cats have always protected fields and granaries from mice, rats, and snakes. Gradually they have become pampered pets, favorite subjects of painters, sculptors, and writers who honored them for their beauty, mystery, and independence, their ability to represent love, fertility, liberty.

But there are always those who fear freedom, especially in someone else. By the early Middle Ages, cats were regarded as evil, consorts of darkness, familiar of witches, and subject to death. So many were killed that the resulting plague (ironically *Black* Death) caused by rat fleas all but decimated the population of Europe.

By the time Jakob and Wilhelm Grimm created the unforgettable Bremen animals, the cat was once more valued for its help in controlling mice and rats. Yet it bore the history of all that "cat" had come to symbolize. Memory is long. The Bremen cat casts a shadow as long as memory. But donkey and dog are comfortable with shadows, will use them, in fact, to great advantage later on in their journey. So they welcome cat and night music into their company. And as the self welcomes each animal into its journey, greater and greater wholeness is achieved.

The three animals continue. Before long they hear a sound in the afternoon that they are accustomed to hearing only in the morning: a rooster, upon the gate of a farmyard, crowing mightily. Donkey wastes neither time nor breath in acknowledging rooster's plight: *Your crowing send chills through my bones. Whatever can be wrong?*

Rooster knows: *I have far too many crows left in me to be put in soup. Because guests are coming tomorrow, I must crow today.* The aborted self. The sense in us that there is more life to be lived. The refusal to go gently into that good night.

The second half of life often meets us with this rooster sense. I am not finished. There is more to me than has ever been seen or dreamed. Much more. As the immediacy of death approaches, a sense of urgency takes hold. I *must* crow all my crows.

As before, the donkey self invites toward the future: *Ah, cock, you are just what we need in Bremen. There we are all seeking something better than death. With a voice like yours, our music will have some quality.* More instinctively than ourselves perhaps, the animals know that old age is not for death. It is for something better than death, for something beyond death. It is for reclaiming the life that leads to fuller life. It is for that which gives life's music some quality.

Rooster's crow pierces the afternoon, clamoring for that quality, in search of the meaning of life's crowing. As does each animal when facing death, the rooster relives the threatened life. What is the rooster side of the self?

Rooster represents the spontaneous self who greets the morning of our lives with zest; rooster knows the moment of birth when we existed in tune with the self. When a baby is wanted and loved and cared for, all the needs of that tiny infant are met. The light shines upon the infant just as the sun rises and brightens the earth. The call of the baby for food, shelter, and most of all love resonates with what is deeply true for the self. That infant knows intuitively what it needs and wants and feels; its "crow" strikes at the very heart of life itself.

Very early the child, to varying degrees, shifts its crowing in favor of the needs and wants and feelings of the caregivers, usually Mommy and Daddy / Mom and Dad / Momma and Poppa. Such changed crowing exists to please or blame or take care of others rather than the self, light years away from the free crowing of the infant. Part of this change involves the child's natural learning to fit into, to find a place within, smaller and larger groups. However, in some cases, the spontaneous crow seems to die out altogether; the sun seems to set very early on the self's true crowing. This kind of phenomenal loss often accompanies the person throughout life.

As our lifestory extends to the Bremen road, our rooster self is the part that sees clearly and responds readily to life's light, even though, as in the original story, rooster spots only a spark in the dark, dark forest. This rooster self is the intuitive response in us to all that is good and right, the spark that can grow to a consuming fire. As we adjust to the demands made on us by ourselves, our caregivers, and society as a whole, our crow may be silenced, dimmed. Yet that rooster self stands on the fenceposts of our lives and perhaps must learn again to take care of the total self — to lead us, to be fearless in staying dedicated to being who we really are and have become since the crack of dawn, the original crow in our lives.

We gather all the rightful pride we have, or at some moment had, and crow with all our might from the depth of who we are. Even when we know, perhaps *especially* when we know, that the fencepost upon which we stand may be near the gate of death, we realize it is never too late to be deeply true to ourselves. We have a message: There is light — the light is within — for ourselves and our world. Oh, rooster, punctuate. Do!

Bursting with the music each still holds within, the four animals set out together for Bremen. Once again the story's truth is simple: No such destination can be reached in one day. Neither Rome nor Paradise. . . . One day's doing precludes the night. No place of destiny, certainly not Bremen, is deserved without a night in the forest and its bed of branches, without the chance to see a spark of light in the surrounding darkness.

So it is that toward evening the animals come to a forest, almost as if the forest came to them. It simply appears within the story. Semi-magical scenery. Instinctively, they know they cannot reach the city of Bremen without going into the forest, this proffered place. The gifts of claiming the fulness of who we are and of seeing new possibilities come when we are willing to spend time, dark time, night time in the forest. There the quiet descends upon us; a kind of inwardness wraps us gently so that we can be with the self.

The old animals are not afraid of the dark. They settle peacefully, and rooster, watchful gyre, stays perched in a treetop. They have each other. In our forest nights, we have our bodies, our faithfulness, our hopes and dreams of Bremen, and our attentive self. In the darkness of the forest, we may be aware of the rejection suffered from others because of our age and lack of "productivity." Rather than focus on society's largely jaundiced view of aging, however, we can choose to be aware of how we may reject the aging process within, a form of self-rejection. Acknowledgment of the aging process, on the other hand, prepares us for the gifts of this stage of life.

In the darkness, even *because of* the darkness, rooster surveys the forest in every direction and spots a spark of light in the distance. That light, we come to realize, is our very self, pristine and whole, present since the dawn of our lives. Hope springs eternal. The animals are awakened by the rooster's mighty crow, their hope enlivened by the thought of a new home, a new place to be. Together they agree to go toward the light. Through the darkness toward the light.

The spark, the light, in their story turns out to be a hut filled with robbers feasting on their spoils. These robbers in the Bremen forest are not hit-and-run marauders, striking one night in a little village and somewhere else the next. They are established, have a hut of their own within a short day's distance of the pastures and cottages familiar to the four animals. All this long while the robbers have been living their parasitic existence, unknown to the animals yet costing them dearly — the shadow side of life, preying upon the supplies of innocent villagers.

We have similar shadow sides. Robbers live within our inner worlds as well, within the forests of our souls, sometimes undetected for many years, draining energy and power from our wonderful animal selves: our donkey vision, our dog faithfulness, our cat capacity to dream, our spontaneous rooster responses to the world around us. Then, in a time of great crisis and challenge, we stumble upon them, led by their light, light that can ultimately allow us to face and transform the robbers encamped within our lives.

How easily overlooked is the small fact that robbers and light coexist in our forests, that our robber selves need light as much as any other self. In a strange and wondrous interplay, our robber selves constantly run the risk, which they are willing to take, of being detected within their forest light. There is something magnetic, something almost seductive about this risk our robber selves are willing to take — as if they *crave* detection. Indeed they do. For within the wholeness of a life, only when the robbers' hidden self is acknowledged, can we truly know our own treasures. In order to fully receive the light, we need to come face-to-face with the robbers within, the indwellers who keep us humble, keep reminding us we are not finished yet, keep us growing and stretching, keep us reappraising the hidden value of what we reject.

Humbly, we see the hut of our life, realize that it is our hut, our home. It is our only place to be with ourselves. The light reveals the robbers who have taken over: robbers of self-rejection, self-hate, self-doubt, insincerity to the self. We see the food of our lives we are allowing them to eat, the treasures of our lives we give them permission to usurp.

How to reclaim when we feel we have given away, bartered, and compromised our very self? The light, the spark we see is unmistakably ours. We know that it is. In this most interior of all struggles, we, like the animals, become one with our selves, summoning all the strength we can muster to take back that which we can call our own.

The four animals decide upon a plan. Together they had set out to make music and this seems a perfect time to start!

Donkey, with hooves on the window sill of the hut, directs hound to jump on his back, then cat on hound, and finally rooster on cat's head. Four become one. The candlelight within the hut catches and magnifies their grotesque, combined shadow on the wall as their music begins, each animal singing a part. Frightened, the robbers believe the animals to be a roaring monster and flee. The once-fragmented self, come to unity, drives out the false self.

After the robbers are gone, the animals feast on the spoils, goods taken from the homes of the countryside in which they had spent their lives. In our claiming what is rightfully ours, we, too, feast on the accumulated food of our lives with its variety of flavors: sour and sweet, gourmet and daily, hot and cold bits. All these scraps — the events, the experiences, the relationships — are ours, and together are wondrous. They may need some looking at, some forgiving, some embracing. But they are truly ours to chew upon, to mull over, to understand, to give insight, to love.

As is so true in our own lives, the shadow side spirals, the robbers return again, believing that they had been fooled and can easily retake the hut. Self-doubt, self-hate, self-rejection and insincerity to the self do not die easily. Despair can creep in. Enticements of busyness, flurries of activities may well invite the false self, the robbers, to return. Inner work, because so profound, takes energy, perseverance, and dedication. Each time a robber self returns as a robber and not as a partner in growth, we need to cast it out all over again.

How can a robber self *ever* be a partner in growth? For sure, not while living hidden and undetected in the forests of our lives. For sure, not if we are unwilling to know at deep, deep interior levels what focus and self-trust are needed to cast aside their ill effects. Yet the robbers guard treasure we might have squandered had we earlier access to it. So it is that the animals teach us how to understand the robbers as shape-shifters within our lives. Ever vigilant and unified, the animals keep the nourishment and treasure side of the robbers' lives, the very dwelling in which the robbers lived, by casting out their threatening surface appearance.

United with their treasure, the animals feast and stay. They make joyful music to the end of their days. So with the integrating self when we welcome and embrace all our powerful, loving fragments, each animal self, each master, each re-formed robber of our hearts . . .

✦

All of us together in a single self —
can a fairy tale ever be so true?

I enfold you, O beautiful beasts,
donkey, dog, cat, and rooster,
as together we journey
out of the skin into the soul.

ii.

The Open Sea

In this body, in this town of Spirit, there is a little house shaped like a lotus, and in that house there is a little space. There is as much in that little space within the heart as there is in the whole world outside.
— Upanishads

It is alarming to feel the soul leap to the surface and find no sheltering wall.
— May Sarton

At the beginning of a short, symbolic year, Hermit Crab realizes that he has outgrown his shell. Filled with both regret and anticipation, he leaves his old, familiar home in search of a larger one. During this move from shell to shell, his "soft spot" is exposed and in great danger. Upon finding a suitable new shell, he begins to decorate, enlighten, and protect it with the help of new friends, only to find that as time passes this shell also becomes too small. After entrusting his beautiful shell to a younger crab and securing her promise to be good to his friends, Hermit Crab sets out once again into the frightening and inviting open sea.

A HOUSE FOR HERMIT CRAB
— Eric Carle

"*Time to move,*"
announces Hermit Crab
at the beginning of this richly sensuous journey
through water, color, and imaginable textures.

Time to move.

Hermit Crab,
can I say it
with any of the assured resilience
you seem to exude?

Time to move.

Is there ever a time not to?
Bewhiskers, my Bremen cat, be with me now.
I want to sit by your fire and dream.
Not move. Definitely not move.

Time to move.

Urgency. I rush forward. But to what? To whom?

Time to move.

Anxiety.   Reluctance.

Time to move.

I've heard that voice too many times in my long life.

Outer voices: Transfers. Graduations. Weddings. Wars.
New houses. New cities. New countries.
Displaced person. Immigrant.

Inner voice: The hidden moves. Heart tremors.
Outgrowing places. Outgrowing people.
The pain of leaving them behind,
of being catapulted past them
with an energy not my own.
Closing down. Backing up.
The endless search for home.
Do I turn my feet to the past
or my face toward the future?
Time to move.

Even as I read, where is there for me to go now?
What path awaits me, beckons me?

Hermit Crab, it's time to move.
Give me a place to stand, and I will move my world . . .

"Time to move," says Hermit Crab one January day.
"I've grown too big for this little shell."

There are natural times to move,
like the seasons and the tides,
and times that are so intimate and unpredictable
that no other earthly eye
could ever sense their approach
or their passing.

Hermit Crab begins his move in January.
A new year for many.
Time of resolutions and indulgences.
Auld lang syne.

How have the journeys of my life been?
What mixture of natural and intimate moves
kaleidoscopes my life?
When has their delicate webbing
ever come into balance long enough
for me to sense a pattern?
What pattern do I sense now?
Is this a period of balance or imbalance for me?
Of movement or stillness?
What do I want to happen with this time of my life?
What is my LifeWork now?

How does Hermit Crab's January move begin?
With a realization that he has grown too big
for his little shell.
Oh, the pain of this!
Children are born being outgrown.
Older siblings walk and talk.
Adults brush low-lying clouds as they pass.
Children long to catch up, to be like the grown ones.
Giants. Heroes all.
And growth happens.
Like Topsy, they grow.
One fateful day,
balance on weightless scales,
they outgrow.

The emperor's new clothes
are no clothes at all.
A sailor falls from grace with the sea.
How can it be that wings do not hold Icarus up?
The earth, the rock-solid earth,
has a scar,
a crack in its seamless surface.
Who might fall through?

Do I remember the first person
who fell through the crack in my life,
the first person I outgrew?
What were my feelings?
Fear, anger, denial, a wish to turn back?
Ouroboros:
I will swallow my own tail,
get back to the womb somehow.
I want my old shell around me again.
What places have become too-small shells for me?
What people and relationships?
How have I tended to react?
Do I stay too long? Move too quickly?
Believe my shell will grow
even as it hardens around me?
Where am I now?

From this vantage point, wherever I am now,
I watch Hermit Crab step out of his too-snug shell
into the fright of the open sea.
The big fish in the open sea.
The biggest fish of all is my fear.

Am I afraid to walk with Hermit Crab
looking for a new house
along the ocean floor?
Am I afraid to go to Bremen?
Am I afraid of the journey
out of the skin into the soul?

Fierce fear,
I will not reject you.
I will embrace you.
I will carry you along with me.
In my new shell I will see your other face,
and you will be revealed to me.
I will know your inner name.

As February dawns,
Hermit Crab finds just the house for his new dreams,
"a big shell, and strong . . .
wiggling and waggling about inside,"
he sees it feels just right.
"But it looks so — well, so plain,"
thinks Hermit Crab.
Hermit Crab has moved
and his reward is in his feelings.
It feels just right.
With a knowing deeper than knowing,
he has moved;
and with a feeling deeper than fear,
he feels it to be just right.
Oh, yes. Amen.
Let me *be* here. Let this be my place.

I have taken the vulnerable journey,
exposed my soft side to the sea.
Left one small shell behind,
and the new one looks . . . plain.
I grieve not so much for its plainness
as for the fulness I left behind.
I allow this grief its month or moment to hold me,
just as fear did.

O holy grief,
you never let me leave
the sacred loves of my life.
For that I thank you
and invite you to move forward with me
to the moment of this plain shell.
Can you sense its very plainness as healing?
Not much yet to distract me from you.

Feeling right/looking plain; feeling right/looking plain.
Yin/Yang. The movement of breath.
Out/in. Over/under.
Peaceful. Prayerful. Plain.
And from deep within that plainness
comes a purification.
My senses are washed, cleansed.
I see my plain house with new eyes,
feel the fulness of life on the ocean floor:
the beautifully swaying sea anemone
to live on my shell,
the handsome starfish to decorate,
crusty coral for beauty,

snails to vacuum, sea urchins and stones to protect,
lanternfish to brighten.
With this beauty and brightness, the rhythm returns.
I grow.
I grow. And I love my growth.
It feels just right.
The sense of well-being surges.
At first, fleeting moments. Gradually, more abiding.
A place. Home. Where the light is.
Warm. Radiant. Reassuring. Hearth to heart.
Let us build three tents. One for you.
One for Moses. One for Elijah.
Here let me pitch my tent.
Here grow roots.
From here journey no more.

"Now my house is perfect," cheers Hermit Crab.

A cheer. A perfection. A lilt of inner joy.
From here journey no more. October thoughts.
Harvest and hallows.
Satisfy the spirits. Pumpkins and bread of the dead.
Pan de los muertos.
Make holy the hidden.
Whose ghost breathes in these unseen winds?
Oh air full of auras! October feelings.

But in November . . .
All saints. All souls.
Communion of saints and commemorations.
Let us give thanks for our perfect house.

But in November,
Hermit Crab feels even this new shell
a bit too small.
I have grown.
Today I pushed against the inside of my shell.
Brush of butterfly wings.
Oh, the hurt of that first hint. Move again?
Face the open sea?
These new friends have become like family.

"How can I ever leave them?"

If I forget you, O Zion . . .
If I forget you, O Zion, as I wander on.
The entrusting time:
Before I go, I care and care for.
Will you love my loves as I have done?
I entrust them to you.
The smaller crab promises to live well and lovingly
in the house Hermit Crab must leave.
Her promise eases the leaving.
Good-bye, good friends.
Good-bye, fair house.
I am not as fearful as when first I found you.
Even though the ocean floor looks wider
than I remembered,
I am not afraid.
With each inner emergence,
the ocean floor looks wider.
An inviting vastness, once fear is overcome.
The path from shell to shell seems shorter.

The open sea offers a new house,
a perfect house,
"a big empty shell."

Once again the emptiness. The perfect emptiness.
Old friend, I know you now. Faceless one.
Or Janus of many faces. Sleight of face.
Would I know you anywhere?
Will you pursue me everywhere?
Oh necessary emptiness, great teacher.
You look into the face of fulness, drawing me.
Hermit Crab's new shell looks a little plain, but . . .

"Sponges! . . . Barnacles!
Clown fish! Sand dollars! Electric Eels!
Oh, there are so many possibilities!
I can't wait to get started!"

Possibilities.
And their power.
What are mine?

O Hermit Crab,
your story is like breath.
Time to move . . .
I can't wait to get started.

Time to move. . . . Wondrously symbolic that Hermit Crab's underwater journey begins with the same intuition as donkey's. Two stories, one wisdom: the recognition (almost a precognition) that it is time to move.

Any journey to Bremen starts in the underwater world of Hermit Crab, with an inner urgency to move. We need to heed this quiet voice. It may be more important than we can ever realize.

With the Bremen Donkey, the stirrings inside and outside give inspiration to leave before being put out to pasture and forgotten. Donkey senses that there must be something for him beyond, maybe Bremen. To get there, though, he knows he must make a move, leave the familiar behind, meet new companions along the way: dog, cat, and rooster. Within each of them as well, donkey enkindles a spark of hope. Yet circled round that spark is a despair, a hopelessness that this is it, the end. Their very first journey, their way to Bremen, like ours, winds along the road of that despair. The world is closing in, the shell of their existence becoming too snug.

Movement is essential to all growth: some asked for, some unsought; some dreaded, some welcome. Hermit crabs know instinctively about movement. They must move when their shell becomes too snug. Although they have a hard skin, their abdomen is very soft and must have protection to survive in the open sea. The crab inhabits successive shells for the express purpose of protecting this "soft spot" from being crushed altogether. During any move, the "soft spot" is exposed for all to see — and perhaps to harm. A most fearful time.

January, in Hermit Crab's symbolic year, reveals him in the midst of this wrenching process of accepting movement as inevitable. Like Hermit Crab, we, too, reach such awareness times. The in-between times — when we know and feel that we must move before what held us in the past crushes us. This knowing time, whose clock may be external or internal, can be a period of exhilaration, a glimpse of new possibilities. Most often, though, it is fraught with anxiety and fear, full of worries: What if . . . ? and, If only . . . and, Why didn't I . . . ? and, How come?

Just such fear permeates Hermit Crab: *What if a big fish eats me before I find another shell?* This fear arises from literally not knowing how we will survive in the unknown. The open sea, like the sea of life, is wide and vast, full of possibilities. Perhaps a forbidding place. A place filled with the wonder of untold beauty — or of destruction, maybe even death.

This fear can take a variety of forms. Some of us may blame ourselves, others, or even the ocean floor itself. Some may be overwhelmed, cry, and feel helpless. Others may experience the ache keenly enough to want to die rather than move. Some of us may try to hide within, saying, "I don't know how to make this move. . . . I don't want to learn anything new." Some may smolder with anger or bitterness.

Held so in the thralls of fear, many do not seem to feel the exhilaration of the possibilities, perhaps can see none *until the move is actually made.* In the letting-go process of movement from one shell to the next, an imbalance is created. During this period, the familiar structures are gone. The emptiness and plainness of possible new shells cannot be denied.

At any stage of life, the letting-go experience can be frightening. As we reach old age, the process is often more dramatically so, perhaps because of the realization that death is closer than ever. Perhaps because we have let go of so much already. Perhaps because there is less need for external stimulation and adventure, aspects of earlier moves that helped make them somewhat easier. The call to move at this time of life often leads to inner directions and growth. Hermit Crab knows this fear as he notices simultaneously the pressure of the snug shell around him and the safety of that very shell.

There comes a time or times in every person's life when stepping out like Hermit Crab onto the ocean floor, into the open sea, is far more total and all-embracing than it has ever been before. The death of a parent, the birth of a child, a move to a new culture where a "foreign" language is spoken, the death of a partner, the loss of a child, the diagnosis of a life-threatening illness, a visit from a loved one long dead — all are moments after which reality, as we have come to know it, may never be quite the same again.

If aging occurred in a moment, it would, no doubt, be one of those times. As it happens, though, aging — in the external form at least — usually slips upon us more gradually: a first wrinkle, an arthritic knee, a few grey hairs. But many can identify some moment more than any other when the reality of aging became a more permanent life fixture and, with it, the need to create new meanings for the self, to bring a rich and chaotic past to bear on the present moment, and to sense some renewed significance for the future. These are central concerns for the second half of life, a time graced by the move out of the skin into the soul.

Hermit Crab's symbolic year of change and growth offers a rich paradigm for this important passage.

In January Hermit Crab steps out, faces his fear. February brings a possibility, a hope. Upon finding a new shell, Hermit Crab becomes splendidly resourceful. The new shell seems plenty big but oh so plain. His task is clear. In early spring he begins to gather a community around him to enhance his life while offering them his friendly companionship in return. So it often is with our "human" shells: We move into a certain emptiness, begin to make a home, and gradually share our lives with the new community around us.

Hermit Crab's shell may be plain, but his surroundings are not. He notices the beautiful sea anemone swaying in the water. He invites them to live with him. They change his shell and he feels better. The starfish and the coral agree to further decorate his home. Reflecting on our shells, we can recall people who came into our lives — some at very plain and painful points — and made them more beautiful. Their beauty forever sways within the waters of our memory.

Creative movement through life requires more than beauty, however, as Hermit Crab demonstrates in June. We need ways to clear the clutter, the pressure, the stress from our present shell. For when we get too weighed down, we are then unable to move. The little snail agrees to help clean Hermit Crab's house, to make room for the new, to keep enough space for the soft spot to live and flourish. Inspiration, insight, and influence from others, books, prayer, and meditation can enable us to stay focused and centered within the growth power of our lives. These gifts can do for us what the lovely little snail does for Hermit Crab.

July turns Hermit Crab's thoughts in still another direction. His new shell is now both beautiful and orderly. Yet still the big fish lurk. Where does Hermit Crab turn for protection? An unlikely source: The spiky little sea urchins come to his aid, establishing balance, maintaining a much-needed distance, preventing any enemy from getting too close. Their limy shells and long spikes add to Hermit Crab's ability to protect his soft spot.

Big fish lurk in the human sea, as well, as we seek both protection and growth space for our soft spots. We never want to be absorbed, swallowed up by another, and destroyed. We are separate, we need to be separate and to know that we *are* separate. While perhaps frightening, the realization of our uniqueness is also most awesome. It lets us know that we are: We are responsible for who we are and who we become.

This is the inner work of the second half of life: becoming deeply familiar with who we are and who we *allow* ourselves to become. Responsibility for the emerging self often manifests itself through both the inner urgency and the ability to stop blaming others for who we have become. Through the presence in our lives of the unpretentious sea urchins who help us maintain our space, uniqueness, and balance, we can continually establish ourselves as separate, involved yet inviolable, entities.

So from March through July, Hermit Crab's life involves decorating, cleaning, and protecting — in a word, incarnating himself within the new environment. As beautiful, as spacious, and as protected as our lives may be, however, the dark times still come, spiraling their way through layers of love and loveliness. That is exactly what Hermit Crab and his friends discover in August when they wander their way into a forest of seaweed. Echoes of the road to Bremen: the sudden appearance of a forest once again. Two stories, one wisdom: Growth needs darkness.

For us, also, the "It's-so-dark-here" and "How-dim-it-is" and "How-murky-it-is" and "I-can't-see" and "It's-like-nighttime" periods have to be faced. In their unpleasantness these times may seem everlasting and we may feel without hope. Many experience deep depression and a sense of being lost. As Hermit Crab discovers, and as each story's wisdom in turn reveals, even these dark times of life usually have the gift of light within them. Lanternfish come and guide Hermit Crab's way through the unknown.

So goes Hermit Crab's journey: from one symbolic February finding of a new shell, to an equally symbolic November noticing that it also has grown too small, and to the December entrusting of it to a smaller crab. Just when everything seems perfect and we feel safe within the boundaries of our lives, we notice that it is yet again time to move.

Recognition of the time to move is not always conscious. Probably most of the time it does not represent a weighed decision. Rather, like the movement of the open sea, it is organic, swaying, pushing life along in its riches.

As always, reflection on the movement from one shell to the next can enlighten our journey. Sometimes, as with Hermit Crab, physical growth starts the process. Or an event, a loss, a development of the mind, the social self, the spiritual self voices the *time to move*. Whatever the impetus, Hermit Crab takes along his body and his soft spot, together with all that he has learned while living in each shell.

While the pressure to move is often external, the development of the inner self does not necessarily follow the same pattern. We can learn deep and lasting lessons from each shell, each life stage, lessons we hope will add to our growth and development. The shells that contribute this kind of nourishment to our interior life are usually those in which we feel safe and loved unconditionally. Some shells, however, make a different contribution. They fail to provide a sustaining environment so that, while there may be external movement, the soft spot stagnates, receives very little spiritual sustenance. Within such a shell the person often lives in shame, guilt, fear, resentment, and carries these feelings along from shell to shell.

Whatever the experience of living in our present shells, the experience of leaving them may be painful or exhilarating — usually both. "He had come to love his friends, the sea anemone, the starfish, the coral, the sea urchin, the snail, the lanternfish, and even the smooth pebbles. . . . *They are like family. How can I ever leave them?*'" All leavings relived in each leaving. The leaving to begin kindergarten or college . . . old family, new family, old job, new job, old city, new city, old self, new self. . . . Each good-bye holds both pain and treasures to enlighten our journey and lend some meaning to the next shell and to the whole of life. Each stage offers lessons to learn, the possibility of growth and potential which, when developed, will enrich what happens next.

Shell after comfort-giving shell becomes too snug. Refusal to move would crush the precious soft spot altogether. As time goes on, Hermit Crab becomes more accepting and unafraid of this movement. With each new shell, more ideas come about how to decorate, enlighten, and protect the soft spot.

Unlike Hermit Crab, we sometimes decide, consciously or unconsciously, NOT to move; we decide to stay put emotionally, socially, intellectually, or spiritually. There is a feeling of safety, perhaps, or of being tired, as with the Bremen donkey. Who has not known the effects of stagnation? However, for Hermit Crab, as well as for the four old animals, not to move would eventually lead to death, whether in the pastures or in the open sea. Our deep human spirit, ever fresh and young, longs for more abundant life, life that can only come from deeper, wider, wiser forms of decoration, protection, and enlightenment.

Most especially during the second half of life, the movement inward can inspire us to live more deeply the meaning of life. There may be great losses experienced: loss of partner, job, house; adult children gone away (or maybe unwilling to be in touch); and, of course, deteriorating health, whether physical, mental or emotional. Old friends die. New friends, it may seem, are impossible to make. The self is scraped skin-thin.

Yet somewhere within the shells of the second half of life comes a momentous realization: The soft spot we carry within from our earliest childhood is itself the place where the light is, the deepest core, the primal prism. The movement of Hermit Crab becomes our movement. We focus on the light within. Tending to it revivifies the soul.

External to us is the loving or not-so-loving world, still important but often without the power to paralyze that it once had. We have learned more about how to care for ourselves. Our journey on the ocean floor of life has taught us. Our succession of shells has taught us. Our friends, the barnacles and snails and sea urchins, have taught us. We can let go. The time has come to pass on what we have learned, where we have lived, to smaller, younger crabs so in need of the shells we have made more beautiful.

As is the way of story, Hermit Crab's journey is symbolically every person's journey. Claiming our shells, learning to love the places we have been, learning to appreciate our lives calls for a willingness to revisit those old shells, to deeply enter each and remember the pain, the joy, the texture, the feelings of each.

Like Hermit Crab's, our lifestories, too, take place in the vast and frightening open sea and in the succession of shells we have chosen to shelter our soft spots. And yet, like most people, we probably have, at best, only a dim sense of the journey of our lives until now: a scattering of memories, some cherished, some wished away; a handful of regrets to balance a handful of hopes and dreams still held, however loosely, to our heart. Like many, we may even question the importance of our past to the life we still wish to create into the future. The past is over; for good or ill, the most important aspect of our past is that it *is* over, indeed, *all over* the present moment, even all over the future.

Our past is our partner in every breath we draw. The present is the breathing in, the past the breathing out. The kind of partnership our past provides depends a great deal on how we carry it with us. At the very beginning of any significant LifeWork, we need to recognize the importance of approaching our past in an ordered and complete way, not in a hit-or-miss fashion.

With Hermit Crab as our guide, we can revisit those abandoned shells of our lives that still echo so loudly — and even those that are quieter — to reclaim both the power and the energy we may have left behind. We can see and visit these shells, past selves, sensing the mixture of natural and intimate moves that led us from one to another. We can bring our lives into balance long enough to sense patterns: patterns of decoration and protection, of enlightenment and darkening; patterns of season and spirit. With keen awareness, we can know that our lives continue to emerge.

The goal of such revisiting is to hold our lives in wholeness rather than in isolated bits and snatches, to heal and clear the memories that devour energy and even hold us captive in some way. From our deep embracing of each abandoned shell, *whatever* it may have held for us, we have the potential to contact undreamed of energy that can free us from hostage-holding memories and allow life-giving memories to deepen and become ever more sustaining.

As we age, many of us experience for the first time — or at least more strongly than ever before — the *need,* not just the desire, to gain a sense of our whole life, its movement and meaning. For far larger rewards than reverie or nostalgia, we want to hold our whole life in all its parts; we want to *re-inhabit* our lives, retrace our path across the open sea to visit each abandoned shell, and then in a wondrous new way never abandon that shell again. Bid it good-bye, perhaps. Welcome it hello, perhaps. But add it to the growing abundance of life instead of growing abandonment.

There are many ways to revisit our old shells, to gather our lives into a whole. Particularly helpful for some is the writing of an autobiography, a process that can provide a structure within which to revisit the places, the shells, we have lived in throughout our lives. Other ways include telling our stories to another, talking into a tape recorder, sewing something, painting, drawing, actually revisiting places or people who have deeply influenced us. In whatever fashion we re-inhabit our lives, attention to this deep inner work provides opportunity to hold our lives as whole, to be aware of places of strength and places of sorrow, to clear up old business.

The various periods of our lives are like old and new shells, different for each one of us, yet bearing some similarities: the family and childhood shell . . . the school years shell . . . the adult shell . . . the shell of the present moment. Smaller shells within these major shells.

With each new move, we set out into the open sea: that wide, vast place of possibilities; that dark, forbidding place filled with the wonder of untold beauty and a hint of horror. Like cat's night music, the open sea represents the unconscious and preconscious possibilities within any life. Deep inside this ocean we move, feeling its movement from within and without.

From the start Hermit Crab's central goal, like our own, flows from the need to protect the soft spot, that part so precious yet so utterly vulnerable when exposed. This soft spot, the very center of who we are, identifies us more surely than any gene or fingerprint. Throughout life, whenever we venture into the open sea, our task is clear: to find a shell to protect our center. Otherwise we know we will perish.

Within our first shell we can discover much about how to care for that tender, fragile self. Utterly vulnerable at birth, we are all soft spot as infants. Almost immediately we find a shell to protect the self. Simple interactions between children and caregivers begin the process of protection or rejection.

When warmth, tenderness, and acceptance pervade the first shell, we usually move easily, delightfully decorating, enlightening, and protecting subsequent shells. Some of us may not have been as fortunate as Hermit Crab. For whatever reason, we may have lacked the resources to make each subsequent shell into a safe, growing place. The open sea may seem forbidding, dangerous. It may not occur to us that there are resources out there to help make our lives, our present shells, interesting, caring places to be. Then the open sea, large as it is, looms like a mine field — so threatening that the shell becomes a place to hide from life, from potential and development. Then the self, the soft spot, stays deeply hidden as we move through life, cringing, joyless, fearful, and resentful.

Whether the first shell has been protective or punishing, reflection on it allows the self opportunity to know its beginnings, to sense early and ongoing *patterns* of response and responsibility. First shells, first houses, first homes become the foundation of knowing, learning how to be within the home, the shell, the self. Those early patterns come to our aid as, with Hermit Crab, we prepare to deeply re-inhabit the shells of an entire life.

Such a task may seem as vast as the open sea or as long as the road to Bremen. It may seem a fearful or impossible risk to revisit, to get *inside*, all those experiences. And yet there, and only there, can we discover the insights of a lifetime. Often past pain blocks entrance to the treasures of a life. Shells that cost us the most — emotionally, spiritually, intellectually, or even physically — may be lying dormant. They may be the very shells that were, or will yet be, the turning points within our lives.

As with Emily in Thorton Wilder's *Our Town*, who is allowed to return to earth after death to look once again at her life, we may be amazed. Emily knows she never realized, never really noticed the wonder of her life: ticking clocks, fresh-cut flowers, warm baths, and warmly ironed clothes. She wonders if it is ever *really* possible to grasp life's beauty while living it.

Reentry into our life story is one way to realize life *while we are living it*. For many of us, as for Hermit Crab, the push to move often came all too soon, just as we were getting settled. There was not enough time to appreciate, to look deeply at what was happening within our shells.

O miracle of midpoints, of second halves! Now there is time, *Time to move inward*, to retrieve the fulness of life contained in the shells of a lifetime.

✦

Possibilities.
And their power.
Where are mine?

O Hermit Crab,
your story is like breath.
Time to move . . .
I can't wait to get started.

iii.

The Ocean's Sigh

However, childhood is neither longing nor terror, neither Paradise Lost nor the Golden Fleece, but maybe it is a horizon, a point of departure, a set of co-ordinates from which the axes of my life may draw their meaning.
— Georges Perec

At every age, in every person, there comes a partial imprisonment, a disabling psychic wound, an unavoidable combination of circumstances, a weakness that we cannot banish, but must simply accept.
— Helen M. Luke

In this African tale, young Bimwili accompanies her two older sisters on her first trip to the sea. While there, she receives from the sea a precious gift: a shell in which she can hear the ocean's sigh. Starting home, she realizes she has forgotten her treasure and returns alone to reclaim it, all the while singing a song about her shell. When she arrives at the ocean, an evil creature, a Zimwi, sits upon a rock with her shell. He asks her to come closer so that he can hear her song. When she does, he grabs her, imprisons her with her shell inside his drum. He makes her his "singing drum." While her family searches day and night, the Zimwi takes her from village to village, receiving food in return for the entertainment he provides with his drum. When they reach Bimwili's village, she hears her mother's voice and directs her song to her mother. Her sisters recognize her voice from within the drum, and she is freed. The next day, the Zimwi, shape-shifter that he is, returns as a pumpkin to devour Bimwili. Once again she is saved. That night she shares her shell and her story with the people of her village.

BIMWILI & THE ZIMWI
— Verna Aardema

Bimwili, Bimwili,
are you sister or self to me?
The music in your name lulls me beyond thought,
rolling endlessly in my ears like ocean waves
to times I can barely touch.

And do I really want to?
Aren't they best left alone,
those primal pains?

My fear speaks its important questions.
Bimwili, I would rather be soothed by your salvation
than accompany you on your journey.
Yet even in this lulling place,
I know that I will never be satisfied
until I, too, become you, Bimwili,
my lost child self,
and return to the dawn of the ocean's sigh,
to my first hearing of it,
to my early weighing of pain and promise,
of gift and burden.

I seek a wholeness.
At this time of my life,
I need to touch and hold you, holy child,
as you then could never have held me.
Strange, isn't it, how we dream of growing up
without ever dreaming of growing old?
You never imagined me,
never saw your older face in the future's mirror,
and so could never be whole
as I have the chance to be by embracing you.

Child self, I speak:
We shall be one.
We shall grow to be one.
The self of now,
the self of then,
and the lost child self of always.
We three as one. Bimwili as our guide.

Early morning.
The mist still pink from the sunrise.
Early morning in my life.
How long did it last?
Who shared it with me?
What color was the early morning of my life?
Who/What was its sun?
Three sisters set out for the sea.

In the early morning I am young.
Others are older:
Siblings. Cousins. Neighbors. Friends.
Sometimes they want me near. Sometimes they don't.
They have done things before, been places before.
They forget.
When they are very young
(but not quite as young as I)
they want to forget,
want to seem older and more experienced.
They forget how long is the path to the sea.
The sea. Place of knowledges and mystery.
Life itself may be a long path to the sea.
We may never be there and always be there.

Sea to shining sea.
Waves and tides and undertow. We the lemmings.

There is no trip like the first trip.
And this is Bimwili's first trip to the sea.
Can I remember the eagerness
of that early morning trip for me?
Wanting the others to want me along?
As I remember, where am I in my life?
What feelings and memories
is Bimwili's journey stirring in me?
The first time . . . The first time . . .
What am I doing for the first time?
The air abuzz with warnings:
You are much too small.
The path is much too long.
Something will befall you.

For what lifetasks have I felt too small?
Whose voice do I hear telling me so?
Who warns that something will happen?
Do they sense the urgency within me
that knows something *must* happen?
Destiny calls like a dream.
And this first trip is so large a part in that destiny.
What sense of my own destiny
did I have as a small child?
How did it manifest itself?
What events gave me hints or clues to my future self?

Wrapped in warnings,
Bimwili sets out on her jungle path

"vibrant with the morning songs of birds."
And so did I.
Who sang my morning songs?
What sound do they have today?

The three sisters finally reach the sea.
The older girls, experienced in the ways of water,
jump right in.
Bimwili plays where sand meets sea,
the water's edge.
The great meeting places of life:
The borders. The boundaries.
The tight ropes. The balancing wires.
Dividing lines. Crossover points.
The water's edge separating before and beyond.
And Bimwili about to enter.
Poised with the gift,
the wave washes in.
A shell like a "daytime moon."

Ai! she cries.
Ai! The unutterable gift
reaches each one of us very early.
Instant recognition. It's mine.
Two child words in every language:
"No" and "Mine."
"No" to begin the distancing.
"Mine" to begin the distinguishing.
The mine that is me. Motherlode.
All my life this one strain of gold.
Deeper. Richer. Wider. More beautiful.

I could not be other.
This shell's song tells me so.
The secret song of my inner self.
My sisters oblivious. My parents oblivious.
What is not hidden but can never be told.
Mine. The beginnings of me.

Bimwili, a daytime moon!
Can you, small girl, ever imagine its significance?
The part the moon will play in your life?
The months. The menses.
Too huge to hold, this daytime moon.
Your sisters, their moons won on some earlier day,
already back to each other in the waves.
You on a nearby rock to examine your shell.
It possesses each of your senses in turn.
Pink insides.
Bumpy ridges. Spiraled peak.
Smooth open side.
And then the sound. The surprise of it.
The sound that calls forth your song.
"A soft SHHHHHH." Quieting, deafening sound.
The sound that calls forth the song
you never knew you had,
never knew 'til now.
Bimwili's song:

> "I have a shell from out of the sea;
> A shell the big wave gave to me.
> It's pink inside like the sunset sky;
> And in it you hear the ocean sigh."

And in it you hear the ocean sigh.
Whatever the gift in any life,
it contains the ocean's sigh, the sigh of the sky,
the moan of the mountains, the agony of the earth.
Sunt lachrimae rerum.
The tears of things.
The crying deep down within.
What is your gift? For in it you hear.
You have always heard. The invisible crying.
The *lachrimae rerum.*

When a child first receives a song,
she sings it over and over,
and hearing deepens, grows more subtle.
When a child first receives a song,
she carries it lightly.
Her substance has not yet become song.
It is still apart from her
and she can set it down,
play elsewhere, as is a child's way.
Not far. On a rock nearby. Not far.
So Bimwili.
The shell safe. The secret self secure.
Bimwili unchanged but never the same.

The morning sun moves to noon.
The sisters start home,
shell still safe on its nearby rock.
Forgotten. Not long. Not far.
Bimwili remembers.
She must return.

Her sisters unwilling. Next time.
Bimwili knows about next times.
Next times are not first times.
Forgotten gifts are not first gifts.
And she takes the biggest step of all.
Alone.

No one else can ever go with the self to its dearest secret.
Bimwili knows she must go.
Alone and afraid.
To the startled jungle eyes she sings her song:
"And in it you hear the ocean sigh."
She sings from swamp to shore.
And stops.
There on the rock with her shell sits a Zimwi.
Creased face.
Arms like an octopus.
Jambo. Hello. Sea waves like snakes.

"I want my shell . . . "

"Sing for me first."

Oh, the Tommy Tucker songs of life!
I do not want to sing for my supper.
I do not want to sing for my shell. My very self.
The song, like the shell, is mine.
I can give it.
If you take what I do not give,
you never have it.
You have a sham song.

A song of shame for your emptiness.
Yet when we are young,
we sometimes do not know how not to sing.

Bimwili begins. Thin voice. Thin knees shaking.
NO! The Zimwi. I can't hear such shaky singing.
Sing it again. Closer and louder.
To save her shell, Bimwili leaves her self.
Brutal barter:
Self for shell. Shell for self. Self for self.
Each child knows this song.
How and for whom did I sing it?
Do I sing it still?
(Remember, I am self and shell and Zimwi.
I am wave and rock and drum.)
I want my shell.
The Zimwi wants me, not me, my song,
what he can wring from me,
what he can gain from me.

Bimwili is close enough to touch her shell.
Oh, this singing can stop!
Whisk. It does.
The Zimwi grabs Bimwili,
stuffing her, shell and all,
into his dark drum.
"Mama! Mama! Mama!" screams Bimwili.
Dark drum of death, second womb,
from its depths Bimwili calls out to her first womb.
Mama! Mama! Mama!
The Zimwi's laugh is her only answer.

He will be fed, become rich, become famous
on her substance, her shell, her song.
World's oldest profession. Usury.

Yet she still has her shell,
still hears its song.
It is only then from village to village
that she truly hears the ocean's sigh.
It has become her own. Bimwili's sigh.
She and the ocean are one.
In her dark drum she is too huge for her sisters,
her mother, her father's search party to find.
They hunt for many days.
Bimwili and the Zimwi walk for many days,
eating jungle food and sleeping on jungle mats.

After those many days,
time and times and half a time,
they come to still another village.
Bimwili unseen,
the drumhead securely fastened over her.
The Zimwi seeks the men in the village circle,
around the mango tree.
He has a singing drum. For food, it will sing.
Food Bimwili never eats.
Food she hears and smells being prepared.
A woman approaches to ask the Zimwi, *Fish or fowl?*
Womb to drum. Her mother's voice!
Tonight Bimwili will sing to her.

"I have a shell from out of the sea;
A shell the Zimwi stole from me.
It's dark in here like the midnight sky;
If you listen you'll hear Bimwili sigh!"

Her sisters hear.
Her mother sends the Zimwi to the river for water.
Her father opens the drum.
Bimwili is free.
The circular journeys of rebirth.
She is once again in her own hut,
newly bonded to her sisters,
and almost free of the Zimwi's power.

In his anger the Zimwi tries once again
to devour her and her sisters.
As they escape, he flies to her rock by the sea
and changes to his usual self.
Kwaheri. Farewell. My little singer.
He releases his hold on her.
She is free.

Free, she has a story to tell and a shell to show.
Within the circle of fires at moonrise,
she sings once more. Sings out of herself.
The same song, Oh! how differently.
Her shell is passed among the people of her village.
One by one, they are amazed at the sound
that unites them.
They are one in the ocean's sigh.
SHHHHHH . . .

The ocean's sigh. . . . Song for the soft spot in the universe. All of creation groaning in travail until now. The tears in things. . . . How full are human words of the grief within the human heart! Shared grief. Communal grief. Known-to-all and all-knowing grief. And, therefore, grief that can be transformed. Purified. Alchemy. The shape-shifter. Grief, the greatest of all shape-shifters. Grief as gift. Grief that leads to the circle of fires at moonrise. To the new shell. To Bremen. Each station of grief, a familiar post on the human journey.

Like donkey, age sends us on a new quest of an ancient, in-buried dream we long to share with others abandoned on the road. Like Hermit Crab's, our shells have a way of becoming too snug, and we sense the movement of our entire lives as a succession of shells. With Bimwili, we are ready to enter even more deeply into that first of all shells, the world of childhood, to rediscover there first gifts and primal beauty, misty morning songs wombed round with night music.

Bimwili's story/journey contains so many recognizable elements — awe, eagerness, solitude, desire for companion-ship, loss, fear, self-squandering, reclamation — a cycle the child within any adult knows, remembers instinctively. With Bimwili, we can deeply reenter that all-important cycle of experience: precious gifts received in childhood inno-cence, the loss of those treasured gifts, the circuitous jour-neys of reclamation, the consequences of seeking or not seeking to retrieve them.

On the journey we share with Bimwili, with Hermit Crab, with the Bremen animals, the next step is to recon-nect with the child self, to summon our inner child forth to release its creative and healing energies within our lives. Some call this "cathecting the inner child," regaining touch with lost libidinal energy, primal energies, life-driving energies. (Those of you who love language may delight in the intriguing connections to cathode, catheter, catharsis, varying kinds of purgations and illuminations.) The work of summoning the inner child is a journey as well, a journey back to the horizon of our lives, to the point of departure, early morning.

As her journey begins, Bimwili is all child, no adult overlays to work through. With the encouragement of her mother and despite the objections of her older sisters, Bimwili eagerly sets out on the long path to the sea. Without knowing it herself, she stands at a crucial point of departure.

That point of departure, those first precious five to seven years of life, hold the kernel of the self. It is during these years that our sense of Who I Am and Who the Others Are develops. These very important years live on in us no matter how old or young we grow.

To gain access to these early years, it is necessary to re-member — in the fullest etymological sense of bringing to *membership,* enfleshing once again — what it was like in childhood to BE. The child is open and in the moment fully present (unless, of course, there is severe trauma). This utter presence without consciousness of time, not thinking of anything before or beyond, makes the child vulnerable in a way that allows the child to feel whole, eternal, and powerful. How powerful, free, and unafraid Bimwili felt in making her request to go to the sea. The sea, the unconscious, is connatural ground for the child. Only we as adults have been taught to fear its dark/bright mysteries.

When Bimwili sets out, she does so with enthusiasm and excitement, all the while having to beg to be allowed to go to the sea. As we face this journey back to Who I Am, we, like Bimwili's older sisters, can make all sorts of excuses not to go: "I'm too old," "I'm too sick," "I've lived my life," "What business have I got looking to the self?" and so on. These words are spoken from very old voices within us — Mother, Dad, siblings — those who consciously or unconsciously held us back or whom we felt held us back.

For persons committed to LifeWork, these old voices diminish in importance. When we make the choice to revisit our childhood shell, we have reached a moment of enormous decision: We have taken a bold step toward proud and responsible ownership of the separateness and connections of a lifetime.

The very request to *go* for the first time begins Bimwili's long path of individuation, her willingness to separate from the ouroboric, unchosen mother, and to initiate relationships from within the center of the growing self. Up to this early morning in her life, Bimwili had known only the connectedness of the undifferentiated self: Youngest child. Baby sister. Tagalong. Now she wants to extend herself outward, to discover what is truly and uniquely hers.

In revisiting the childhood shell, we, too, may sense how the balance between separateness and connection, self and communities, works out in our lives. For some of us, there may be an untapped urgency to establish or reestablish a sense of a separate self. We may feel that we have never really taken that significant journey to the sea, have never left our earliest shell, have not gone to enough inner places alone. Others of us may sense we have lived too much alone, too isolated from others, have never felt the solidarity and support of Bimwili's circle of fires. The energy we discover in our childhood shell may give us the direction toward individuality or involvement that we most need.

We can summon our inner child in the hope of touching within those warm, wild, and ultimately welcoming, waters some memory that will let us know the "I," the self, in its pristine freshness. Bimwili walks in that sheer delight to the sea, even though her sisters, who know about time and danger and tagalongs, do not want to take her. From this day of Bimwili's life comes the experience she will have for always: playing by the seaside, finding her beautiful shell. Free, free to be, and free to interact with her world.

These memories last a lifetime. Yet in our busyness, we can learn to forget such moments. We sometimes learn to forget ourselves, learn to function from the adult world — often a place of collective forgetfulness of the inner child. We lose our freshness of vision, our spontaneity, awareness, autonomy, and ability to be intimate with ourselves and others. The child in us retreats, becomes neglected and rejected.

We need always to recapture the power of childhood play, to re-member some time in our lives when we "just *were*," when the inner and outer child rejoiced in wonder at the world. I re-member such a time. I grew up in West Texas under the enormous sky. One Saturday evening after my bath in the old metal tub, I put on a hand-me-down, ankle-length, flowered robe and went out into our dusty yard and danced mightily for the cows who stood in awe of my antics. I remember the vast sky, the rhythm of my body, and the fulness of life. I was whole and vast and all of everything.

Bimwili's experience exactly on that first walk to the sea — whole and vast and all of everything. To her, as to her sisters before her, the sea issues its magnetic call whose meaning cannot be wholly known to her then, only felt. Like a dynatype within her life, destiny begins to unfold. There is an *inner insistence* at work. Inexplicable. Inexorable. Fierce fidelity to the unfolding of her own life — even before she knows it is unfolding. Destiny drawing her like a dream. The child already held, cradled within forces so much larger than herself. Realities far beyond the personal, begging entry and shelter within the heart of a child.

Each child knows, and knows deeply, intuitively, such mystical morning songs of life, no matter how violently subsequent years might distance the self from the song. Not only does every child know such songs; every adult can reconnect with them. That linkage forms the central core of our second half LifeWork. Song to song. Donkey's dream of musicianship.

Bimwili passes through a jungle vibrant with her morning songs and so reaches the sea. Her older sisters jump right into the water. Not so Bimwili. She plays at the water's edge, foreplay to the future. Before entering the water, Bimwili must know the boundaries and their blending. The place where air meets earth and earth meets water. Stillpoint of the turning world. Because at that very point, the universe is constellating about her, pregnant with the gift about to be born. A moment of immense power for Bimwili.

Tumbling in upon a huge wave comes something resembling a "daytime moon." Bimwili acknowledges, is astonished by, the specialness of the moment. Ai! She emits a cry of joyful recognition. The shell, overwhelming gift of the big wave, is intended for her.

Bimwili stands identified to the universe. A gift. Mine. A gift that defines me, gives me my denotations and connotations. A gift that situates me — to myself, to a world larger than I can now imagine. This marvelous play at the edges forms the real work of childhood: being open and available to the gift. Equally marvelous is the play of age as we do our real work, the same work in different form: being open and available to the gift.

What is the relationship between a life and its first fruits, its first gift? Often, as is the case with Bimwili, a flash of instant recognition. Ai! A seizure of spirits. The soul knowing for the first time its innermost secret: that part of the self that can be given but never totally spoken because it exists in a world both before and beyond words. Bimwili's shell awakens her senses with color and texture. Like a daytime moon, it gives her some foreshadowing of womanness, of sexual identification. And finally it imparts its song, her song:

"I have a shell from out of the sea."

Primal gifts, such as Bimwili's shell, always proceed from subterranean waters, deep recesses of the unconscious, and connect the self back to its origins within those waters, the sea.

"A shell the big wave gave to me."

The receiving life, in this instance Bimwili's, always acknowledges the giver. Throughout history, the giver has been variously identified as big wave, fire sun, earth mother/goddess, father god, great spirit. The giver is big (wave) and connected to an even bigger unnamable unknowable (ocean). Young as she is, Bimwili acknowledges the generous love of something much larger than herself.

"It's pink inside like the sunset sky.
And in it you hear the ocean sigh."

Most mysterious of all! When children receive their life-gift, they receive both the power and pain of the universe. They become *cosmos-capable*, able to identify with worlds way beyond the self, not in any figurative sense, but as literally as they choose to actualize such capacity within their lives. Most cultures have known and accepted children as natural mystics. In the final line of her song, Bimwili exemplifies this time-honored knowledge about children.

Yet, so like any child, Bimwili holds her gift loosely. It has not yet become her substance. That, after all, takes a lifetime. With her shell safe on a rock, she continues her play in the water. Who knows but that she may even have been searching for further shells.

High noon reaches all morning songs. And for Bimwili, the sun's height means the journey home and, midway there, the remembering: My shell! But sisters reluctant to take Bimwili in the first place are even more reluctant to take her back. No one ever realizes the total import of a child's first gift except the child. As much as others may nurture and care, there comes a time when the child has to go alone and risk all to guarantee the gift — exactly what Bimwili does as she makes her fear-filled return through the jungle to the sea.

All too soon, the consequences of her risk become apparent. Surrender of her song. Captivity. Reacquaintance with the gift in darkness. Perched on the rock, long arms encircling *her* shell, sits a Zimwi. He entraps her with the very gift she identifies as the center of her self. Perform. Prove your right to be special, to have received such a gift in the first place. Bimwili sings to get it back. The shell is hers; it *is* her. And then she is taken and held captive. From there the dullness sets in: *Thud, thud,* says the drum while the little girl sings her forced song.

For most of us, there was a time when we, too, were taken captive by the big people in our lives. There was a time when we felt diminished and, for some, even a time when we felt we no longer existed. The pain of recalling such early memories is great. It may seem pointless to those so traumatized, difficult to believe there is wholeness anywhere. Destroyed as we may feel at many levels of life, at the center of our being — very likely only at the center of our being — *we can find ourselves intact.*

How to find our way back to that center becomes our most important LifeWork. Hesitation, reluctance at this juncture need no justification. We know the journey involves passage through a dark, robber-infested forest, across an open, possibly hostile sea, within an airless drum. Fear overtakes us as it must have Bimwili, hidden away in the drum and made to sing her song at someone else's whim.

For many of us, the selling of our personal song took place in less dramatic ways than being locked in a drum. Abandonment of the self, of the child within, occurs when we discount what we *know*, what we *feel*, what we *need*, and what we *want*. Our drum may have been that of silence, confusion, appeasement, uncomplaining endurance. When we are little, we are willing to do almost anything because we are so vulnerable. Our caretakers are big physically; we are small. They are strong; we, weaker.

When trauma occurs within the family, adults are so caught up in the difficulties that they often fail to convey necessary information to children. Because the thinking capacity of children is not developed, it is difficult at such times for them to process information. They may then draw incorrect, although unconscious, conclusions, such as, financial difficulties are my fault; or, it's my fault Daddy and Mom don't get along. This illusory sense of power convinces them that, by being bad, they can magically make things like divorce, illness, or death happen.

The other side of this tragic fallacy is that children may believe that if they are really good, everything will magically be okay. They may decide that *good* means to be quiet, or helpful, or overachieve — whatever will please Mom and Dad. The Tommy Tucker songs.

Conversely, children may rebel and react to stress in a "negative" manner to get the attention of caretakers. Either way, this attention is of the utmost importance. Children will sacrifice all to attain that attention, as important to the young self as Bimwili's shell is to her.

At times children may block out what is going on because the stress is so great. If such denial persists, children grow numb inside and stop feeling what they actually feel, substituting instead feelings that seem acceptable in the situation. Instead of feeling anger, which well may be the appropriate feeling, children may grow fearful or even sad. The joy so natural to children then is replaced with a dull thud of sadness or recurring fearfulness. From her early morning freedom to her early afternoon captivity, Bimwili undergoes just such an inner undoing.

When stress becomes overwhelming, children have few options. They cannot decide to move or leave or make grownups hear. At this most vulnerable stage, children deprived of understanding and parental awareness choose one of two alternatives: adaptation or rebellion. Each can be imagined within Bimwili's story.

Bimwili finds herself trapped with her precious shell inside the drum of the Zimwi. She is little; he is big and powerful. He says sing; she believes, rightly or mistakenly, that compliance is her only alternative. She must sing so that the Zimwi will be pleased and fed and — ultimately — yield a few crumbs to her. Bimwili adapts to her understanding of her circumstances.

Well-meaning, loving, and caring as parents are, they are very human. In their humanness and need for pleasure, they sometimes encourage children to believe themselves captive. And the child concludes, "I must be who my parents want me to be. I must sing when they say sing or when *I* *think* they they say sing." Certainly children can incorrectly decide that parents require a specific way of being, thinking, and feeling.

While Bimwili did not choose to react to her entrapment by rebelling, she could have. *That* Bimwili would have kicked and screamed and refused to sing. For such behavior, we can only imagine what the Zimwi would have done.

Rebellious children, just as surely as those who adapt, give away what they know, feel, want, and need. Although they garner negative attention, they rarely get needs met. Such children are punished, sometimes excessively, without any recognition of themselves as persons. Either way, by adapting or rebelling, that most precious gift — the gift of self — is surrendered.

And yet, as with Bimwili, both the song that is ours, the song of the self, and the song of the shell resonate with a single truth: "I shall always be." No matter the pain, stress, adaptation, or rebelliousness, the kernel of the self remains intact. Our work in the second half of life is to become aware that, at some point, we became captive, gave ourselves up, stopped thinking our thoughts, feeling our feelings, and knowing what we wanted. To reclaim the original song of the self, distant echo though it may seem, we *can learn* to get back to the center and be the unique, one-of-a-kind human being we are.

Through the very process of re-membering those early years, shedding the unshed tears, expressing the intense anger, and confronting the worst fears, we come face-to-face with the self. With care-ful, committed LifeWork that most

precious self comes flooding back irrespective of the intervening years, in fact all the more precious for its long
absence.

With Bimwili's initial reception of her shell, the surface
contradiction arises that *within* the gift resides the burden,
that *because* of the treasure, captivity follows. All shining
has its shadows. If the shell had not been so precious to her
in the first place, the Zimwi would never have taken root in
her life. Gift and burden. Wonder and wound. For children,
much of the tension inherent within their central gift involves the challenge of integrating it with the other people
and circumstances present in the same life.

For Bimwili, the Zimwi represents in story fashion the
sum total of opposition — from herself and others — that
her gift will encounter, all of what she will have to discover
in order to share her gift. The Zimwi embodies all the
jealousy, suspicion, entreaties to compromise, attempts at
usury, temptations to charlatanism occasioned by the presence of such a spectacular shell in so young a life. Bimwili's
first lesson is to sing for her shell. What she received so
effortlessly from the "big wave," she must then work to
maintain within her life. In most lives this lesson includes
some form of successive withdrawal into darkness.

So powerful is the *knowing* within great stories that
each detail has metaphorical significance. When the Zimwi
grabs Bimwili, he just happens to have beside him the
drum. The darkness that enters our lives does so with
exactly the right tools for our enlightenment. After he stuffs
her into the drum, almost as an afterthought, the Zimwi
tosses in the shell. Even *within* darkness, she has her
precious gift. In fact, forced as she is to sing, Bimwili learns

much more about her shell than she ever could have by just playing at the seashore. Darkness precludes distraction. Fear gives focus. Only during her dark trip does she come to realize her union with all that is outside her, all that is *other*. The ocean's sigh becomes her own. Her song evolves: *"If you listen, you'll hear Bimwili sigh."* Intimate identification. My sigh is the world's cry. All who know, however vaguely, the union of self and spheres of stars will hear.

For Bimwili, who is the listener? Her sisters. They are the instruments, the companions, the accomplices of her captivity as well as her release. Ongoing bonding of women. Intricate. Intense. Multi-dimensioned. Bonding so threatening to patriarchies. Once heard by her sisters, Bimwili activates both "female"/imploding and "male"/exploding energies — her mothering self, her fathering self — to secure her freedom. She garners forces from within and without to rid herself of the parasitic presence.

At that moment, she becomes more than herself, more than her shell, her gift. Her very substance becomes song and spirit. Her personal gift transforms itself into a gift for others. Within the circle of fires at moonrise, empowered by the eternal symbols of circle, fire, and moon, Bimwili sings again. The same song, Oh! how differently. In night music all are united.

Her shell is passed to each villager. Each pair of hands holds it. Each heart hears its echo of the ocean. They are drawn not so much because it is Bimwili's story but because, in the force of her telling, they feel their own lives reflected. The villagers hear not Bimwili's song, but their own; imagine not Bimwili's story, but their own; hold not Bimwili's gift, but their own. Bimwili's story unites her listeners in the power of a single shared story with multiple manifestations. All become one in the ocean's sigh. The ultimate mystical experience is communal.

Like Bimwili, carried from village to village to her home village, we, too, will finally come home to the self. We will hear the voice of a loving Mother/Father, our own inner-most voice, that part of ourselves that nurtures and gives us permission to be, to be free. That inner voice can be sparked by various external persons or events: a class, an old friend who re-members us, a life-partner, our child, a dream, an old photograph that yields a memory. We feel lifted from the captive drum.

We are home. We have begun the long journey out of the skin into the soul. The dawning of that realization is like nothing else. Other wants pale in relation to this deep self-recognition. We can and will be invited away again, just as the Zimwi comes again in other forms to claim Bimwili. We can be invited away by activities, consumerism, feelings of victimization and blame, even by retirement itself. Yet, as we come to *know* our home place, it becomes increasingly impossible to wander far. We know that the cyclic journey in darkness spirals once, twice, many times: Zimwi-like shape-shifting within a life, deepening the story that life has to tell, the unifying witness-power of the life's wisdom.

Most wonderful of all, we become able to share our story, our gift. Before we reach some degree of freedom from our captive drums, we ourselves are unable to hear what our story is telling us. No sharing is possible. But release from captivity means that our ears are opened. In telling, we hear; in hearing, we tell. We become one with all who know the ocean's sigh as their own. SHHHHHH. Sound of shared awe.

✦

Within the circle of fires at moonrise
she sings once more. Sings out of herself.
The same song, Oh! how differently.

iv.

The Old Stone Wall

. . . however blind, unbalanced or one-sided a man or woman may be in youth, [s/he] will be saved by the one essential quality of the inner life — devotion. . . . This object of devotion will carry . . . a projection of the hidden and often quite unconscious awareness of the Self.
— Helen M. Luke

And this is what a poet
Is, children, one who creates
Sacramental relationships
That last always.
— Kenneth Rexroth

Frederick, a field mouse, lives with four other young mice in an old stone wall near an abandoned granary. As they work diligently storing supplies for the approaching winter, the others chide Frederick for his apparent idleness. Frederick busies himself with a different kind of work, gathering the memory of the sun's rays, the color of the seasons, and the words to express these gifts. In the cold of winter, after the nuts and grains are gone, Frederick shares his "supplies." The cold, hungry mice are enlivened and warmed by his words. They name him "Poet," and he shyly accepts what he already knows about himself.

FREDERICK
— Leo Lionni

All along the meadow of my life,
the meadow of my life,
the meadow of my . . .
All around the mulberry bush,
the mulberry bush,
the mulberry meadow,
All along my life,
all around my life,
there is an old stone wall.

Wonder wall.
Weeping wall,
spite wall,
mending wall.
Windowless wall,
windowed wall,
wall to wall to shining sea.
Wall to the future,
wall to the past,
wall to this moment's meaning.
Wall to transcendence,
wall to transparency,
wall to the daily sacrament.
Wall of separation,
wall of inclusion,
wall of illusion,
wall of wisdom.

From the meadow of my life
I contemplate the wall.
Old friend.

Its craggy features so like my own.
I run my fingertips across its brindled surface.
Nooks and crannies of more history than my own.
Keeper of cows and horses,
guarantor of their grazing.

All along the meadow of my life
runs the old wall.
Setting limits.
Creating wonder and desire.
Suggesting beyond
and inviting me there.
Beckoning wall,
reckoning wall,
wall of blessings.

Within the wall,
near the barn and the granary —
the abandoned barn and the empty granary
at the approach of winter —
Frederick and the other mice have their home.
Their home, their storehouse.
Their old stone wall.
Small mice chattering and gathering.
Corn. Nuts. Wheat. Straw.
Chattering:
We work. We work.
Why aren't you working, Frederick?

How to respond?
The hidden work.

The silent work.
The inner work.

I am working,
Frederick answers.
The lonely work. The long work.
The LifeWork.
Gathering sunrays for winter days
both cold and dark.

The other mice, incredulous:
Our arms ache.
Our muscles are sore.
Surely you can't . . . .
You are sitting.
You are staring at the meadow.
Even the Bremen cat
could catch a sitting mouse,
a staring mouse.

I am collecting colors
to paint our winter world,
says Frederick simply.

Simplicity.
I sense the winter behind the winter.
I feel the cold beyond the corn.

Dreamer.
Are you sleeping while we work?

Oh, no!
I am wrapping myself in words
to wear for the winter.
Oh, no.
The only one awake.

And soon the winter comes to all their gatherings.
Corn. Nuts. Wheat. Straw.
Rays. Colors. Words.
White snow upon the wall.
Peaceful protection of their plenty.
Lots to eat. Stories and happiness.

You see, Frederick,
say the other little mice,
our work is the real work after all.

But little by little,
nibble by nibble,
their work dwindles.
Nuts. Berries. Straw.
Only a memory of the mound
of yellow corn.
Scraps and silence.
Cold and the chattering of tiny teeth.
Memory?
Memory . . .
Isn't there something else to remember?
Some gathering that does not dwindle?

What about Frederick's supplies?
What about his storehouse?
The storehouse not contained in this old stone wall.
The storehouse not measured or seen.
Frederick climbs upon a stone,
large and round,
part of the wall
around their winter.

Close your eyes,
he says to the others.
For this kind of seeing
eyes must be closed.

Slowly he sends them
rays and colors and words.
Now Frederick alone has open eyes.
His work of inner seeing
spreads filament by filament
to the inner storehouse
of the others.
The glow. The warmth. The rays.
Frederick sharing his storing from a winter rock.
Bimwili sharing her story at moonrise.
Within the circle of fires,
sharing what a life has stored.
Atop a pile of stones,
sharing what a life has stored.

Is it the speaker's voice?
Is it magic

that so creates what was never here before,
that so warms the other little mice
from the fires of Frederick's life,
that colors their world from his inner landscape?

Little by little,
golden glow by blue periwinkle,
small warmth by painted color by rich word,
Frederick opens the treasures his life has stored:
Treasures of being and seeing and holding.
Treasures of sorting what is precious
and offering it outward
to the storehouse beyond the single self,
beyond the old stone wall,
beyond all limits and times.

Why, Frederick, "you are a poet!"

Still shy and blushing,
Frederick receives his life name,
the name of what has been stored
in the old stone wall
along the meadow of his life.

"I know it."

I know it. . . . Precious words. How the human heart longs to hear them, to speak them. To know and be known. Longs for a moment in which to *know*, even as we are known, to know precisely *because* we are known. A moment that makes the examined life worth living. That forms a community of knowing. A coming-together of knowingness. Within the cloud of unknowing encircling any life, how can such knowing be reached as comes to Frederick at the end of his story?

The answer lies with the paradox at the beginning: old stone walls. The beginning of the story finds Frederick in a place where everyday happenings occur. Cows graze and horses run. Mice glean. There is a meadow, to be sure. What life has not known a meadow, place of peace and playfulness? Along the meadow, however, runs the old stone wall.

Like Frederick, we, too, live our lives within parameters, often not of our own choosing. Parameters that may seem crushing or comfortable, perhaps a little of each. Within the wall of life, we are born and grow and change, get stuck and survive. The amazing reality is that within these confines, whatever they may be, we *claim* ourselves. In fact, the more familiar we become with the boundaries of our lives, the greater the possibility of transcending them and experiencing our connection to ourselves, to others, and to our world.

The Bremen animals, Hermit Crab, and Bimwili have already offered many insights into the nature of old stone walls. In each story, the characters first knew and accepted parameters and limitations and then tested them for all they were worth. What knowledge do donkey, crab, and Bimwili share with Frederick about accepting partial, unavoidable imprisonments? What do they show us about what exists *beyond* simple acceptance?

Donkey and companions know rejection; they know age. Tired bodies, reduced work loads. Unavoidable. Requiring simple acceptance. They know ruthless masters and a youth-addicted society in search of broader, stronger backs. Here acceptance stops. Here vision and creativity begin: They accept the parameters of age but not those of desertion, injustice and despair. Along the stone walls of their pasture runs the road to Bremen. Choice operates *within* their very limitations. Each animal, in turn, chooses to leave the pasture for the path. As they become empowered by this exercise of choice, greater and greater freedom opens before them.

Hermit Crab likewise knows constraint. A shell closing in. Parasites and predators in free-flowing waters. What of his circumstances must be accepted? What must be overcome? Growth itself is Hermit's wall. The natural cycles of expansion and contraction. To continue to grow, he must move, must risk. Inescapable rhythm.

Hermit Crab's move shows two aspects of energizing acceptance. What he must accept and cannot avoid, he does — not grudgingly but with great largesse: He gives over his old home intact to the younger, smaller crab. Then he conducts his search for a new home with imagination and hope: He cannot wait to begin! Granted, not every wall of our lives can be as eagerly embraced. But the ability to *distinguish* between what must be accepted and what can be overcome rewards us with a dynamic toward the future that can be the first gift of old stone walls.

Bimwili's wall, her drum, represents what happens within life in those periods that come to each of us, periods when growth and movement seem stifled, stalled. Our "wall" may be that we feel we are going nowhere, stuck in a rut, backsliding even. Bimwili clutches her shell gift in darkness and endlessly repeats her song, possibly not even noticing the subtle changes that take place within that song, the wonderful way in which the ocean's sigh becomes her own. In dark repetition she gathers momentum to transcend the limitations of what seems to be her fate.

Like Bimwili's drum, some walls are temporary and can be outgrown within the maturation process of life. But all walls can be gifts. Life expands — and reaches the challenge of a totally new parameter. Without a new wall to bump against, we might never know our next inner task, never realize how our spirits will be stretched.

As we face our limitations, noting the mistakes we have made, seeing where we have compromised our truth for whatever gain — through greed, lust, hatred, anger, cowardice, dishonesty — we let ourselves know the meadow of our lives and our surrounding wall. Every craggy, stony piece. Every color, every season, every storehouse, the cold and warmth of life. As we claim each piece, each piece becomes our own. We truly *re-inhabit* our lives, not in a figurative or fanciful sense, but with a deepening awareness of personal history and reality.

With Frederick, we become ready to re-envision the re-inhabited life, to search for and see deeply what our life has stored, the *under*knowledges, the *under*gifts, the *under*contributions, the lost or hidden legacies, the unsuspected riches. Frederick, whose life is very ordinary, even, by some standards, dull. Frederick, who, in fact, does not produce at a par with others, who has a damaging effect on the bottom line, the small animal GNP. Frederick, who could easily have measured himself by external markers and given up. In our frantic-paced, twentieth-century world, Frederick's name is legion, his story illustrative of our personal and collective stories. So how do we read his story, our own?

Along a meadow. Within a wall. Frederick shares his harvest world with grazing cows, running horses, butterflies, and purposeful ants. With four other little field mice. His family. Full of fall. Autumn in their air. Seasonal storing about to begin.

But this time, all seems different. Since the farmers moved away, their barn and granary no longer yield food and winter warmth. No corn-filled crevices. No animal breath to dull the chill within the stables. This year the field mice themselves must orchestrate their own survival. And so they do. Busy day and night — except Frederick. Small bones already sensing winter's approach, already responding to external demands and circumstances — except Frederick. Perfect picture of industrious midlife. Time when the ageless scale weighing being and doing, creating and producing, often tips toward the more measurable, more overtly essential forms of accomplishment.

What, after all, is Frederick *doing*? His companions chide: *Why aren't you working, Frederick?* How can Frederick explain? The pain of being different. So connected, yet different. Frederick senses his inner work is equally important to them all. But they *see* what they are producing. Day by day amassing supplies. Stackable.

Countable. Accountable. How can Frederick validate the invisible, highlight the hidden?

So it is with innermost gifts. Many gifts have been surrendered because of negative judgment on the part of others, judgment that often leads to self-doubt and disparagement. Some gifts are condemned so early in life that they lay buried for decades, almost forgotten even by their owners.

Frederick hears his gift labeled laziness, dreaminess, doing-nothing by his busy companions. Yet he does not capsize under the weight of their criticism. In a language they cannot yet fully understand, he defends his work as parallel to theirs, as equally necessary for the long winter ahead. While they gather nuts, corn, and straw, he gathers sunrays, color, and words. His work is directed to the same end as their more quantifiable work. It is Frederick's work, however, that will transform their winter isolation and hunger, that will be expanded rather than depleted when shared.

Early winter seems to confirm the busy belief that external storing is all that will be necessary. The little mice have plenty to chew on and chatter about. Stories of silly cats and foolish foxes. Outwitting. Outwaiting. A mouse's world of pride and prowess. But, true to its nature, winter perdures. Stone walls are colder than barns or granaries. Stories and seeds grow scarce. Outer hunger gnaws a memory: Is there, after all, another appetite? Who has spoken of it?

In their midwinter crisis, the four companions turn to Frederick. Did he mention something once about supplies? Could he produce them now? Until he is called upon in such dire circumstances to use his gift, Frederick may or may not have known its power. When he is asked, however, he knows no hesitation. He climbs onto a big stone within their wall. The barrier becomes his ballast. He acts and directs from a core deep within himself.

Frederick knows exactly how his supplies can be shared, can be used to call forth inner supplies the other mice never realized they have. The key lies in his directive: *Close your eyes.* Turn. Move from one level of reality to another. Look inward. Discover there what *your* life, not just mine, has stored.

No matter what our stories, like Frederick's brothers and sisters, we, too, have been *storing* at deep, unconscious levels. Many of us may have gone through life with no conscious memory of our gift, no memory of our storehouse ever truly being seen, singled out, recognized by an other. If our gift was mentioned at all, it was discounted. Yet the presence of a single Frederick within a life evokes untold wealth, as the little mice soon learn. They ask for his rays, his colors, his words. Frederick speaks "as if from a stage." His gift is his connection, umbilical cord to the beyond. Frederick disappears and a larger presence unifies them all. His gift, his long-stored, life-stored supplies spill over, warming the other mice, brightening their world, transforming them, easing their transition from exterior to interior realities.

Perhaps we, too, have known such electric moments. Music. Commanding orators. A stunning sunset. A memorable moment of ritual. Even a great tragedy or disaster. Moments that elicit tacit knowing. Knowing such as comes to Frederick's family when they give him his name: "Poet."

Still shy and blushing, Frederick acknowledges ownership of that name. The KNOW of his "I know it" is the untranslatable, intimate knowing of *yodah, wissen, connaitre, conocer,* the knowledge that exists in blood, breath, and bone. At such a sacred point, if only for a brief moment, self-knowledge, power, and humility become one. Knowing his name in this deep, inner way, Frederick can then name others, can call forth their inner storing as he has already begun to do.

Frederick's story represents the transition between the first and second rhythms of LifeWork, between *re-inhabiting* and *re-envisioning* a life. Donkey, Hermit Crab, and Bimwili teach us much about the first rhythm. Then along comes Frederick, a simple field mouse, to say that each of our lives contains treasures of interior strength and creativity if we only learn to look with new eyes, indeed *closed* eyes.

Doubts come easy: "Yes, I have a life. BUT it's ordinary. I don't think I could possibly discover any larger or deeper patterns and meaning in my life. I mean, I am what I am. I'm not a poet like Frederick. I'm not a musician like my sister, not even a good cook. My life has been so hurly-burly for so many years that I've never really had time to store anything. It has been surface, surface, surface. I think I'm one of Frederick's busy companions and, believe me, the old supplies are long gone."

This discounting voice could echo from any one of us. Surface reality consumes tremendous energy during the young and middle adult years. Like Frederick and his family, we must gather corn and nuts and wheat and straw. During these years, we find ourselves in the midst of focusing on relationships, developing careers, raising children, actively making our mark on the world. Yet Frederick is there as a constant reminder that such work by itself is never, can never, be enough. In earlier adult years, when we eagerly gather material supplies and overlook our need for inner sustenance, our Frederick voice may be very faint. Gradually, a shift occurs.

For many of us, this transition begins about midlife. In women, the change may be dramatically marked with the onset of menopause. For men, there seems to be a turning to what is more personal in life. However the shift happens, its signpost can be ignored. Rooster could have missed the spark in the forest and led the others pell-mell into the darkness. Failure to recognize the time to risk and move could have crushed Hermit Crab's soft spot or kept Bimwili indefinitely within the drum.

Without Frederick, the other mice, too, may have missed the grandeur of their very ordinary lives. For them, as for us, Frederick represents the part of living that is reflective and inward. In our later years of life, an inner voice, our own, invites us to work deep within. This work is often denigrated by the distorted belief that there is nothing left in old age but to wait for illness, loneliness, and death — or mightily try to avoid the reality of loss and mortality. Recognizing the richness of an inner focus is a major task for our LifeWork, and Frederick is busy moving us deeply into it!

Throughout his life, Frederick has been devoted to seeing what exists beyond sight, hearing echoes from the other side of silence. In our lives, such devotion may take the form of interest in music, gardening, carpentry, bird-watching, coin collecting. . . . Ultimately, whatever the source of devotion, it blends with and becomes the "place of bliss," in Joseph Campbell's sense, becomes indeed devotion to the unfolding of the deepest self.

Such devotion to the self, to the inner life, holds the key to preparing for any winter. Sitting next to the old stone wall, gathering and gathering his life into his hands, Frederick prepares ever so surely for the winter of his life and the oncoming seasonal winter. He works. Yes, he works! He works with the cycles of nature, storing sunlight against the oncoming darkness.

Quietly, he sits, and the other mice think he is simply staring or dreaming. He is not! He is gathering the colors and words of his life into a magnificent whole.

Like Frederick, we, too, can silently gather our lives, taking in and feeling, experiencing the fulness. The magic returns. In the wholeness of a life lived and acknowledged, our vision of ourselves kaleidoscopes into patterns and themes not seen before. We see "the story" of ourselves: The drama has been played, the poetry written, the melody shaped. The crescendos and decrescendos become obvious. Time for reflection provides space to learn to feel at home within the meadow of our soul.

Our meadow grew with gifts external to it: the sun and rain, the wind, the four seasons, even the rocks from glacial ages. While living within these boundaries, we grew, developed with (or without) love and support from others. As the first snow begins to fall, we, like the five little mice, take to our hide-out in the stones. At first it is the abundance of external work that sustains us as well. Plenty to taste and talk about. Laborers reaping the worth of our work. Relieved for our rest.

But gradually, as supplies dwindle, we might be even more relieved to go back to gathering. Up against our parameters we bump — nothing is left to do. No amount of scurrying about now will fill emptying coffers. After a time we may feel all the supplies have run out. There is not much to say.

When the other mice reach this point, they remember what Frederick had said about his gathering. They turn to him. And he is ready. It is time to give back with the noblest of all gifts: being who I am, simply BEING.

How to BE? How to be in the winter of our lives? Possibly Heschel's most quoted line — "Just to be is a blessing. Just to live is holy" — begins an answer. Creatively, in our own way, we can share our supplies, what our lives have stored: the fruits of our inner, most demanding and disciplined of all work.

We learn what Frederick knows: that reflective, inner work is liberating, does not diminish, indeed spills over to others. It sees beyond appearances, sees the unseen, feels the future. It knows what to gather *in addition to* external gathering. It has great patience, no need to see immediate results. Nor does it force itself upon the different, seemingly more limited vision of others. It knows its own time to share, responding to both the felt and expressed needs of others. It does not foster codependency but elicits the work of others, their creativity, within its midwifing function.

We are gentle as we prepare to share the overflow of a life lived. *"Close your eyes,"* says Frederick, as the family of humankind gathers metaphorically around his stone, our stone. We no longer preach and demand, nor insist upon our point of view. Rather, as we experience our fulness, the fulness of all humanity is there for us to see and know.

Our lives speak truth. Little by little the treasures of our lives can be given. Insights of a lifetime — mistakes we made, successes we enjoyed, tears we shed, losses we endured, joys we shared, requests we made for forgiveness — all stand naked to be received. In the moments of gratitude, of care for those we have created, adopted, embraced, struggled with and loved, our fulness stands. The seasons of our lives can bring comfort to those who hear and understand. They can give courage to those who lose heart.

In our sharing, as in Frederick's, the magnificence of who we are shines forth. We recognize ourselves. And we are known by others. As the field mice listen with hearts glowingly warmed by the color and texture of Frederick's life and presence, they applaud and exclaim: *"But Frederick, you are a poet!"*

The great gift we can, in turn, receive is to be acknowledged for who we are as we share our life journey. As others see us more clearly, they can name us, just as the mice name Frederick, "Poet."

For his part, Frederick needs no false humility, no disclaimers. He answers simply, *"I know it!"* I knew it in a glass darkly all the while we were gathering. As we come to know our inner names, we likewise tremble with the magnificence of our selves, with the knowledge that *we are*, that we are known to others through the sharing of the self. That at long last we have found a person who both speaks and hears those precious words: *"I know it!"* — and that person is our very self.

✦

Gathering that does not dwindle.
Work of inner seeing.
Storehouse beyond all limits and time.
I know it.

V.

The Field of Flowers

Jacob pulled his hands together in the shape of a small bowl. "Samuel, our life is a vessel, and a vessel is formed for two functions. One is to hold" — then Jacob flattened his hands as if he were making an offering — *"and the other is to pour."*
— Noah benShea

How is there space in the skies for the souls of all the departed? Because, says Marcus Aurelius, they fuse one with another: they burn and fuse and so are returned to the great cycle.
— J. M. Coetzee

As a young girl, Alice, later called Miss Rumphius, lives with her artist grandfather by the seaside. She watches him carve figureheads for ships, helps him paint skies in his pictures; and he shares his stories of faraway places with her. She assures him that when she grows up she, too, will go to faraway places and then live by the seaside. He tells her that she must do a third thing: Make the world more beautiful. In her adult life as a librarian, Miss Rumphius accomplishes the first two tasks. She "travels" in her books and then in many exotic lands, making friends as she goes. When she hurts her back, she decides it is time to find a home and live by the sea. As she grows old and sometimes ill, she finally discovers how to keep her third promise to her grandfather. She buys five bushels of lupine seed and spreads them along the highways and byways. They blossom, and the Crazy Lupine Lady, as Miss Rumphius is then sometimes called, leaves the world more beautiful, inspiring her great-niece to do the same.

MISS RUMPHIUS
— Barbara Cooney

How many names
your life has given you!
Alice.
Granddaughter.
Miss Rumphius.
The Librarian.
That Crazy Old Lady.
Lupine Lady.
Great Aunt Alice.

The circular path of your life.
Alice to Alice.
Dust to dust.
Ash to ash.
Granddaughter to Great-Aunt.
Joining the chain.
The Lupine link.

As I see your life unfold,
I feel my own.
Its search for connections.
With you
I retrace your steps,
feeling my own.

I know you were not always old.
Nor was I.
Once upon a time . . .
How we sailed upon that time!

Once upon a time
you were a young girl
in a city by the sea.
From your porch stoop
looking out at the masts of tall ships.
Looking back at the ships
that brought your grandfather here.
Looking forward to the ships
that would carry your life away.
Figurehead on the ship of your life.
Perched each moment
between BEFORE and BEYOND.
Feeling the past.
Feeling the future.

From your grandfather's basement,
painting the skies.
From your grandfather's knee,
painting promises for your life:

Yes, Grandfather.
Like you, I will travel
to faraway places.
On the map and in my mind.
Outgrowing old shells
and crossing the open sea
in search of new ones.
Grandfather, your shells
sheltering me.
Your basement.
Your ships.

Your paintings coloring my dreams.
Your life teaching me.
Your life.
Your legacy handed over to me.

Grandfather,
like you, when I am old,
I, too, will come to live
beside the sea.
Near the ships.
Near the shells.

My young eyes are opened.
My young heart is stretched.
Grandfather speaks from his long life:

"There is a third thing you must do."

In my youth
how can I do more
than vaguely sense
this third thing?
An artist's words:

*"You must do something
to make the world more beautiful."*

Oh yes, Grandfather!
When I know what that is,
I will do it.
But I do not yet know

what shall be revealed to me,
what my life will unfold.
I must yet live the meantimes.
Washcloths. Porridge. And schoolwork.
So I grow,
and so my childhood passes.

Good-bye, good shell.
I leave to seek my life.
And I find it
in libraries and far-off lands,
in green coconuts and mother-of-pearl shells,
in the hearts of fishing village kings
and in my own heart.
And so my life builds itself,
each event and experience
remaining in my heart.
Buried treasures.
Mountains with unmelted snow.
Jungles and deserts.
Friends I will never forget.
Lions and kangaroos and camels.
My first promise to Grandfather:
I will travel to faraway lands.
An odyssey of my own.
Wandering afar
in the middle years
of my life.
Stretching out and returning home.
And home —
never the same.

My home gets built up as I do.
Self by shelf.
Until one day,
like Odysseus centuries ago,
I come to the Land of the Lotus Eaters.
Lotus,
sacred flower on a spindly stalk.
Magic flower.
Magical food.
Take and eat.
Those who do
forget — at least for a time — their homeland
and the ties of family and friendship.
Those who do
find their home
in their heart.
Those who do
remember their first home
and become home everywhere.

And then,
one camel
in the Land of the Lotus Eaters —
getting off his back,
I hurt my own.
Just as suddenly
I know it is time
for my second promise:
to find my place by the sea.
Waterworld.
Great unconscious ocean.

Great ocean of unconsciousness.
Womb of beginnings.
Ocean of origins.
What shall I learn
in this place by the sea?

I shall watch the sun come up,
watch it cross the heavens
and sparkle on the water.
I shall see it set in glory
in the evening.

I shall plant a garden in the rocks.
Seeds in the stone by the sea.
Seeds of myself.
Stone of myself.
And —
between the growth and the gravel —
"almost perfect" happiness.
A nice world.

Yet Grandfather's face . . .
and Grandfather's voice.
And my promise to his memory:
I shall do something
to make the world more beautiful.

As I dream of doing,
my body has dreams of its own.
Dreams of undoing.
Dreams of being.

I, who traveled so far,
am now confined.
This back. This bed.
Bounded by a nutshell
and queen of infinite space.

From my window
I see the lupines.
Blue and rose and purple-colored.
The ones I have always loved the best.
I wish I could plant some more this summer.
But I am not able to do.
To plant.
To scratch stone.
To multiply my lupines.

From the bedroom window
I watch the hard winter.
All sign of my doing disappears.
Only moles see seeds under snow.
My 'I' turns to ice.
Does all doing diminish so?

In the hard darkness,
only pain.
Grandfather,
did you suffer so?
How did I never know?

Ah, sweet knowledge!
Solidarity of sorrow.

Is this solidarity the strength
that makes the world more beautiful?

Grandfather, I know now.
I am with you.
Arm linked to arm,
life to life.
Confirmed I stand.
Connected I stand.
And connections swirl around me.
A vortex of vision.
The ice melts,
and I am not the same.
Spring returns.
My back is better.
And I walk.
Walk.
Walk in wonder.
I am *with.*
WITH.
And the with is WE:
how many grandfathers, grandmothers,
how many great-aunts,
how many shamans,
how many saints?
With you.
I am with you all days,
even to the ends of the earth.

I walk up and over the hill
where I have not been in a long time.

I walk in wonder.
Lupines.
Lupines I never planted.
Blue and purple and rose-colored.
How many winds,
how many waves,
how many birds,
how many earthworms
must have helped?

And then I know,
know with crazed clarity,
what I will do.
Bushels from the best seedhouses.
Five bushels.
Two loaves and five fishes.
Twelve baskets of fragments.
Pocketsful of lupines.

The sower goes out to sow her seed.
Some falls on highways.
Some on country lanes.
Some by schools. (Will they ever know?)
Some by churches. (Will they ever believe?)
Some by old stone walls.
(Will Frederick's friends store it for the winter?)
Some in hollows.
The sower and her seed.
The Crazy Lady.
That divine madness.
Instant insanity.

And the beautiful flowers grow.
Along highways and lanes.
Near schoolhouse and church.
In hollows and old stone walls.
Her third promise to Grandfather,
beauty growing out of the sickness,
the dark, the cold,
and into the communion.

✦

Now Miss Rumphius is very, very old.
Magical white flower
on a spindly stem.
I am her great-niece Alice.
My friends think she is the oldest woman
in the world.
Maybe she is.

We come in slowly at her gate,
and she tells us stories of faraway places.
But she doesn't *look* faraway.
She looks *into* us.

Great-Aunt, when I grow up . . .

And Great-Aunt repeats to me
what Grandfather said to her.
Three things to do.
Three promises.

All right, I say.
All right, Great-Aunt.
All right, Great-great-grandfather.

"But I do not know yet what that can be."

Ahh! the field of flowers! How did Miss Rumphius do it? How to get from birth to here! Each aspect of the human journey sheds light on that important question. The Bremen animals tell of reclaiming life in advanced age. Hermit Crab details the *process* of life passage, the progressive outgrowing of shells throughout life, regardless of age. Bimwili portrays childhood, a childhood symbolic of the entire life journey in all its cycles. For his part, Frederick represents adult responsibility for hunting and gathering, providing and replenishing supplies, while indicating at the same time what else a life must store, what else we are responsible for at every stage of life. Because Miss Rumphius embraces the wholeness of life, she gives us a chance to reconsider each life stage with a slightly new perspective.

Miss Rumphius has a childhood common to many of the world's children until the rise of today's more isolated, highly mobile families. She lives her childhood close to her ancestors and older people. From her front stoop, young Alice sees replicas of the sailing ship that brought her grandfather to that very wharf. Her sense of history, her place in its flow, develops out of her connection to the past. Anchored as she is, Alice does not depend on the newest fad or fashion for a sense of self.

As she paints skies with her grandfather, she participates in significant endeavors with the adults and older people in her life. How many of us have known an attic or basement room filled with smells and smiles specific only to itself, a place made special by the older person who shared it with us! In her grandfather's basement workroom, Alice drinks in his life and dreams, which slowly become her own. Painting skies with him, she envisions faraway places of her own and a future home by the sea.

But during the fire-fed evenings she spends on her grandfather's knee, he insists on a third thing she must do. This she cannot envision: Exactly what might it mean to do something to make the world more beautiful? She makes her promise, though her young heart is not yet capable of imagining what she will do.

Sufficient only that the seed be planted. And in young Alice that seed roots itself early and very deeply — deep enough to grow with her throughout a lifetime, calling her forward to keep her word to her beloved grandfather.

What is significant about life's deep promises is that they are carried out within the normal, daily parameters of that life. The life does not lose its grounding. Even though her heart holds these magnificent promises, Alice still lives as a young girl of her time: eating, washing, doing chores, finishing schoolwork.

The language of story has a special phrase for this: *in the meantime.* In between time. Bridge time. The surface life continuing while energy consolidates at the depths. Kairos lying in wait to burst in upon chronos. Life is more decorated, perhaps, with *meantimes* than with *once-upon-a-times.* It is the meantimes that carry us forward, preparing us for the move from one shell to the next.

So it is with young Alice. Her childhood passes. Goodbye, good shell. Soon she leaves her grandfather's house and city, its sea and salty air. She assumes work that sustains her "productive" adult years. As a librarian, she nourishes and extends the first of her promises, to visit faraway places — first by reading about them and then visiting them. She begins to store vistas, friends, and adventures, all the while understanding, like Frederick, that winter days ahead may be dark and long.

Her winter begins unexpectedly. On one of her trips, she injures her back, an injury that causes her to reflect that it might be time to keep her second promise, to find her place by the sea. The external event of an injured back signals her time to move. Yet so closely interwoven are external and internal events within any life that Miss Rumphius' back may well have been only an outward sign of a "Time to move" that she was already sensing inwardly.

Deep within, Miss Rumphius knows this must be the time, time for her to withdraw from faraway places, to draw within. For her, the back injury, enforced from outside herself, leads to the inner transition to her second promise. Remember what an unexpected snow day may have meant to us as children . . . or the sudden dark of autumn evenings, the pulling-in times? No matter how active a life, the second half of it offers more such drawing-in times.

Each life senses this inner movement, knows something deep and inexpressible about itself: a secret dream (Donkey), an inner stirring (Hermit Crab), a treasured gift (Bimwili), a self-affirming name (Frederick). Such knowledge most often exists at the unconscious ("sea") level of the life, only occasionally leaping to light in rare moments of self-actualization and grace.

Miss Rumphius' story gives clues to the significance these inner times and knowings hold. Her three promises show the clear, necessary life progression from external to internal activity:

The promise of youth:
  I will travel to far-off places.
The midlife promise:
  I will come to live by the sea.
The life-crowning promise:
  I will make the world more beautiful.

I will travel to far-off places, extending the self outward as I go. I will tend, tend to the external sheep of reality's flock. The first promise to travel broadens horizons, expands parameters, gives the self both substance and center around which to grow. Seen in this light, the second promise to settle by the sea is an option for balance, for stasis, so the great inward journey may begin in earnest. Certainly inward work is necessary during the first half of life, and outward work does not stop as one grows older. But in the second half of life, the emerging self knows more about where and when to shift emphases.

So it is for Miss Rumphius in her time to move to the sea. Again in the elegant simplicity of story language, we are told, "And it was, and she did." Just as with Hermit Crab, her momentous passage is not accomplished without pain. She prepares to leave a richly decorated life to enter an empty cottage by the sea. "Feeling right but looking plain . . . "

After a very active youth and adulthood, she may well wonder what it is she will *do* by the sea. From here, travel no more. Her doing undergoes the seachange. Shape-shifter. She will *watch* the sun come up, *watch* it cross and sparkle, see it set. She will place herself in juxtaposition to life's greatest rhythms and cycles. Become one with them. Fuse. Light and sparkling dark. Seasons. Sea and land and intervening rocks. And out of this deep seeing, she will plant. Within the world of her second promise, she is "*almost perfectly happy*," almost . . . because the fulfillment of her third promise still remains a mystery for her, an ever-present underknowledge. Truly, how can she make the world more beautiful? She still does not see.

In her house by the sea, Miss Rumphius is forced to her bed. From the stony ground, a garden grows even as a deeper seeing yet becomes necessary. From her window she can see the flowers she planted before her illness. How she wishes to plant more! Confined as she is, she has only her memories and her Bremen cat as company. What did Grandfather mean? How did he *know* that one must make the world more beautiful?

And in a simple bed in a house by the sea, the answer comes as gift to Miss Rumphius. Lying on her injured back, she understands at last what she has inherited, the transgenerational presence and significance of her grandfather at the beginning of her life and of her great-niece at the end. She becomes the Lupine Link in an awesome chain that stretches from ancestors/progenitors to descendants. Yes, Grandfather. Yes, Great-Niece. I want to be a part of what you are a part of. I want the circle to be unbroken.

In a rush of realization during the deepest part of her diminishment, the vision comes: solidarity of suffering. She is *one* with her grandfather. In his life he must also have suffered in ways she as a child never knew. Now in her house by the sea she is like him. The sweet knowledge of union with the life's beloved — which is always *beyond* the beloved. WITH is what Miss Rumphius discovers. A simple preposition embracing all language.

In, out, up, down, over, around and about have all been left behind. WITH becomes Miss Rumphius' reality. Through her grandfather she touches, lays hold of the procession of grandfathers, grandmothers, shamans, and saints fused in the skies, the souls of all the departed. She lives both *within* and *beyond* herself, rich and broad blood coursing through her veins. Her individual, separate existence is shot through with luminous, numinous presence. Great mystics throughout history have described this experience, birthright of every human heart. Like Miss Rumphius, when we recognize the connectedness created by such solidarity, we gain both strength and a sense of serenity and well-being far beyond the ordinary. The self slips imperceptibly and joyously from *I* to *WE*.

This transition takes place for Donkey as he offers to the other animals the invitation to Bremen. Each animal in turn joins the wondrous *WE*, making the unique contribution that only each self can give. Their communal strength makes possible the envisioning and creation of their shared future.

Hermit Crab forms a *WE* in his world in two different and important ways: first, by leaving the old shell to a younger, smaller crab; and second, by creating an animate and animated social ecology through the decoration, enlightenment, and protection of each new shell. How he loves the barnacles, the eels, the seahorses even when they exist, as they do in the planning stages, only in his imagination.

Bimwili learns in imprisonment what Miss Rumphius learns in sickness. The ocean's sigh, which became Bimwili's, then becomes the vehicle through which her family and village reach a new sense of communal grace. One by one all become one within the sound of her shell.

Frederick's ability to pass from I to WE closely resembles Bimwili's. While her gift is symbolized by an object, his is presented as the fruit of his inner work, his storing. In truth, we all store our stories. That is, in the end, what we each have to share. Frederick's story enlivens the innermost place of each of his industrious, blustery siblings because, through all their criticism, Frederick believes that the creative place of inner work exists not only in himself but in them also. True mystics know that no gift is so singular it resides in only one person. The *source* of the gift, however that gift might be felt or described, and not the isolated self, is the center of *communion* — union *with* the other.

While little Alice did not know what it could be that she could do to make the world more beautiful, old Alice, old Miss Rumphius allows herself to focus and wonder what it will be. She is not unlike ourselves. We may not know how — or it may not even have occurred to us until now — to leave the world more beautiful. We may have considered leaving a mark on the world through children, grandchildren, humanitarian donations and gifts, through work — all commendable. Yet measured against the deep resonance of an ancestor's words — still insufficient.

Pondering those words of her grandfather, Miss Rumphius sees her world and thinks it is already "pretty nice." She enjoys the beauty already present. But Miss Rumphius knows, intuits over a lifetime of echoes, that her grandfather's words go deeper. Earlier, she had simply planted lupines around her cottage to add to the beauty of living by the seaside. She had planted because she wanted to, she wanted to enjoy.

But after the long winter of her illness, she rises from her bed in a burst of transgenerational creativity. She gets out and walks in the spring, only to discover that nothing — none of us — lives in a vacuum. The lupine seeds have been scattered by the wind and the birds to other places. Their beauty — our beauty — simply spills over and beyond. Magnificence swells within, without. The idea takes root within her. Understanding is granted. Miss Rumphius knows what she must do to keep her third promise.

She sends for the very best seeds, five bushels, no less. An extravagance takes hold. Only the finest, the distillation of a lifetime. And easily, gracefully she spreads them wherever she goes.

Truly the Crazy Lupine Lady is out of control. Her carefreeness delights us. She cannot be herself enough! Her back heals. She heals. And each year more lupines grow. More beauty. Miss Rumphius spreads the seeds. She has undreamed of help: the wind, the birds, the rain, and the lupines themselves producing ever more seeds.

As the story draws to a close, Miss Rumphius, very appropriately, is visited by children. They think she is very old. She tells and retells the story. And always the story repeats: I will go to faraway places when I grow up. . . . I will live by the sea when I grow old. . . . But for us, as for Miss Rumphius, that is not quite enough. In her life-won wisdom, she reminds the children of the third thing one must do with a precious life: Create beauty.

The children are fascinated with the old Lupine Lady. To her wise counsel they answer, *"All right."* And we, too, each say all right and then look out into our world and ask ourselves: "What flows out of me to my world?" Our answer, like Miss Rumphius', blossoms forth in the fruit and flowers of our lives.

✦

Seeds in the stone by the sea.
Seeds of myself.
Stone of myself.
Between the growth and the gravel,
I shall do something
to make the world more beautiful.

vi.

Beyond Bremen Town

I would ask you to remember only this one thing. . . . The stories people tell have a way of taking care of them. If stories come to you, care for them. And learn to give them away when they are needed. Sometimes a person needs a story more than food to stay alive. That is why we put these stories in each other's memories. This is how people care for themselves.
— Barry Lopez

I hope you will go out and let stories happen to you, and that you will work with them, water them with your blood and tears and your laughter till they bloom, till you yourself burst into bloom. Then you will see what medicines they make, and where and when to apply them. That is the work. The only work.
— Clarissa Pinkola Estés

Once again on the road to Bremen.
Is there — after all —
any other road?
How different the sand,
how different the sandals
now on this road.

Each animal myself.
Each shell myself.
Each shape-shifter myself.
Each stone wall myself.
Each lovely lupine myself.

On my way to Bremen,
I have crossed the open sea.
Boatless.
No anvil. No anchor.
Naked I came onto this road
out of the sea.
On my way to Bremen,
I have seen the inside of darkness,
have sung for someone else's supper.
On my way,
I have stored seeds and planted seeds,
been poet and painter,
heard echoes of ancestors
and of worlds unborn.

The forest floor is dark again
as I make my way
to the hut where my robber selves live.

How many names I have given
the robbers within!
Big fish. Zimwi.
Cold winters.
Bad backs.
Other, always other.
On this journey I have learned
your real name:
each robber myself,
each shadow only myself,
the dark side understood
and accepted at last.
So intimate your name.
Name to my nakedness.

Prodigal robbers,
I have robbed you!
All this long time and times and half a time,
I have chosen not to see your true face.
And now I do.
So humbling is your beauty.
You are really soft spot and shellgift.
You are poetry
and the beginnings of beauty
and what I have it in myself to do
to make the world more beautiful.

You are there before Bremen.
You, the almost-arrived.
Thresholds.
Points of potential.

The bud to the bee
as much as the bee to the bud.
Converging vectors.
The pregnant pause.
The ripeness that is all —
or nothing.

You call me beyond Bremen
to my furthest limits and stretching,
the wild blue yonder.
Further, deeper, unimaginable.
Piercing through to the heart of creativity,
birth in darkest stillness.
Round yon virgin,
mother and child.
The self as mother to its child.
In Bethlehem,
house of bread.
In Bremen,
the unreached unreachable,
the necessary and miraculous mirage
from within whose mist
emanates a very substantial future.

And out of that mist
what is true —
Bremen need never be reached,
can never be reached.
It will always remain the reached-for.
True to its destiny,
Bremen will always call me beyond.

For Bremen is not a destination,
but a dream.
When I set out on the road to Bremen,
it changes, as does any dream.
In going to Bremen,
I need always to go *beyond* it.
Path to Bremen.
Breath to Bremen.
I breathe
and become my breathing.
I breathe and become all breath.
All breath breathes Bremen:

Donkey, dog, cat and rooster,
master and robber,

                        breathe Bremen.

Hermit Crab and all my shells,

                        breathe Bremen.

Bimwili and my only shell,

                        breathe Bremen.

Dark drums,

                        breathe and pray.

Frederick,
all my brothers,
all my sisters,

                        ora pro nobis.

Oceans and stone walls,

          breathe Bremen.

Fields of flowers,

          breathe Bremen.

Miss Rumphius,
all my grandfathers,
all my grandmothers,
great-aunts, great-nieces,

          breathe Bremen.

All my descendants,

          breathe Bremen.

All my forebears,

          breathe Bremen.

All you great and glorious dead,
          breathe Bremen.

All you grace-filled living,

          breathe Bremen.

Together
on the road to Bremen
and beyond,
we breathe
out of the skin into the soul
and are welcomed home.

Appendices

LifeWork Exercises

This section of the book provides some ideas for further work with each chapter. The exercises will engage you in experiences other than reading. They access the unconscious processes through breathing, walking, writing, sorting, and other forms of creative work.

This work is designed for the individual as well as the small group. Each exercise is intended to take twenty to thirty minutes. As insights and understandings come, welcome them with gratitude and without judgment whether you are working alone or with others.

You may wish to read a chapter and turn immediately to the exercise for that chapter. Or you may wish to read the entire book before working with the exercises that appeal to you. Whatever you decide, enjoy and be playful with these pieces of your work.

Several exercises suggest the use of colored pens and/or colored paper. If you are unable to obtain them, use of a regular pen or pencil and white paper is fine.

Prior to each set of exercises, you will be referred back to the Deep Breathing Exercise on the next page.

May each of these exercises help you to move
OUT OF THE SKIN INTO THE SOUL.

Deep Breathing Exercise

- Sit with your spine straight.

- Uncross your legs and ankles unless this feels too uncomfortable. If you prefer, lie down with arms at your sides.

- Close your eyes as you become aware of your breathing.

- Begin by breathing in slowly to the count of
  1 - 2 - 3 - 4 - 5 - HOLD.

- Breathe out 1 - 2 - 3 - 4 - 5 .

- Take several more deep, cleansing breaths before returning to normal breathing.

- Then begin the chapter exercise you have chosen.

i. Before Bremen Town

Gathering All Myself

PREPARATION

You will need:

- **Five colored pens or pencils.** Select one color to represent each of the four animals and one color for yourself.
- **Four sheets of paper**, large if possible

EXERCISE

- Begin with the Deep Breathing Exercise on Page 165.
- Then place the four sheets of paper in front of you.
- On the first paper write "DONKEY" in the color you chose for him.
- On the second paper write "DOG" in the color chosen for Dog.
- On the third paper write "CAT" in the color chosen for Cat.
- On the fourth paper write "ROOSTER" in the color for Rooster.
- Begin your work by noticing which animal appeals to you. Take the paper with that animal's name on it and set the others aside. At the top of that paper with the color you chose for yourself, write the question:

WHAT DO YOU HAVE TO OFFER ME?

- Set up a dialogue with that animal something like this:

  DONKEY: (Use his color.) I am just here. Inside
  me, I carry a vision of something beyond.

  ME: (Use your color.) I have no idea what you are
  talking about, but I will listen.

  DONKEY: To hear me, I ask that you quiet yourself.

- Continue the dialogue back and forth with the animal
  until you feel finished. During this work, do not censor
  anything that comes to you. What you write is for your
  eyes only. Allow the words to flow.

- Then take your color and write a second question to
  the animal you have chosen:

  WHAT DO YOU NEED FROM ME?

- Dialogue with the animal on that question until you
  feel finished.

- Spread all the sheets before you again and let another
  animal come forward. Again, write the above questions
  with your color and "let" the animal respond using its
  color. Set up a dialogue.

- Repeat this same procedure for the other two animals.

- When you feel finished, fan the four sheets out in front
  of you to thank the animals for what they have given
  you. You may possibly wish to record in a notebook or
  journal any insights you have gained from this exercise.

FOR GROUPS:

- Divide into twosomes and share any insights you feel
  comfortable sharing.

ii. The Open Sea

Visiting and Re-visiting Our Shells

PREPARATION

You will need:

- **Four colored pens or pencils**
- **Four sheets of paper,** different colors if possible

EXERCISE

- Spread the sheets of paper in front of you. Take some time to be quiet by doing the Deep Breathing Exercise on page 165. Be deeply aware of breathing into the whole of your life and breathing out what you need to let go.
- Then choose a pen and a sheet of paper. Draw a shell to represent your childhood world. Label that shell. Ask yourself the following questions and write responses on your paper. Allow yourself all the time you need.

WHAT WAS MY LIFE LIKE IN THIS SHELL?

WHAT WAS I LIKE?

WHAT WERE MY FEELINGS AS I LIVED IN THIS SHELL?

- Choose another color pen and another sheet of paper. Draw a shell to represent your school-age shell. Label it. Answer the same three questions for this shell.
- Choose another color pen and another sheet of paper. Draw a shell to represent your adulthood shell. Label it. Answer the same three questions for this shell.
- Choose another color pen and another sheet of paper. Draw a shell to represent your present shell. Label it. Answer the same three questions — but in the present tense for this shell:

  WHAT IS MY LIFE LIKE IN THIS SHELL?

  WHAT AM I LIKE?

  WHAT ARE MY FEELINGS AS I LIVE IN THIS SHELL?

- As you finish, spread the four sheets in front of you.
- Thank the shells of your life.

FOR GROUPS:
- Get into threesomes and share one of your shells.

iii. The Ocean's Sigh

Early Morning

PREPARATION

- Silently prepare to go for a walk by doing the Deep Breathing Exercise on page 165. Let your breath connect you to the whole of yourself. You may wish to take a notebook or journal with you on your walk.

EXERCISE

- Choose a walk that fits your physical abilities and mood. As you walk, imagine yourself as a little girl/boy. Keep your senses open. Allow yourself to find something in nature that symbolizes the inner life of your child self — a twig, a rock, a leaf, a weed.
- Pick it up and hold it in your hands. Notice the shape, size, texture, and color of the object. Turn it over in your hands. Allow it to speak to you. For example: *"I am a weed. I grow just about anywhere. I don't need much space to take root, etc."*
- You may wish to sit and write the words in your notebook.
- Take the object home and let it become a symbol of you. Make a special place for it. Honor the significance of this gift with song, dance, painting, poetry, a prayer, or simple quiet time.

FOR SHUT-INS:
- If you are unable to go out or are bed-ridden, allow your eyes to wander around your room or outside your window. Let your child self choose an object from outside or inside. It may be a cloth, a book, a flower, any object.
- Notice the shape, size, texture, and color of the object. If you can, hold it in your hands. Allow it to speak to you. For example: *"I am a book. I have interesting ideas inside me. You have to open me to know me,* etc." You may wish to write these words in a notebook.
- If you can, make a special place for it. You may have a conversation with it each day. Honor the significance of this gift that is you with a poem, a song, a drawing or painting, a quiet prayer. Or even do a little dance in bed with your toe!

FOR GROUPS:
- Place a cloth or scarf in the center of your group. One by one, each person who wishes may place the chosen object upon the cloth, sharing with the group how it is a symbol of the self.

iv. The Old Stone Wall

Harvesting a Life *

PREPARATION

You will need:

- **A cup of mixed dry food pieces,** the more varied the better — beans of all kinds, grains of rice, pasta of every shape and color
- **A notebook and a pen or pencil**
- **A large piece of cardboard or poster paper** *(optional)*
- **A cleared working surface, desk, or table top**

EXERCISE

- Begin with the Deep Breathing Exercise on page 165.
- Then pour the dried food pieces on the table or on the large paper. Allow their casual chaos to represent all that you have stored in your life. Sense how huge and multiple your life is, far beyond your power to comprehend or encompass.
- Begin to move the pieces around. See what patterns emerge with the pieces. Some seeds may hold more significance for you than others. Some may represent pain, some joy. Let the seeds speak to you as you sort through what you have stored in your life.

- When you have finished, you may wish to glue your seed "sculpture" to the paper as a reminder of the patterns within your life, or you may wish to place your seeds in a cup or special container.
- Perhaps you could prepare a blessing, a prayer, or a poem to recite over your seeds, your life. You may wish to put them in a special place or spread them on the earth.

FOR GROUPS:
- Place your seed sculpture or your container of seeds on the table. Read your blessing, prayer, poem, or say a few words over your life.

* Adapted with permission of The Putnam Publishing Group from *The Search for The Beloved* by Jean Houston. Copyright © 1987.

v. The Field of Flowers

Legacies

PREPARATION

You will need:

- **Five colored pens or pencils, magic markers, or paints**
- **Five sheets of paper**

EXERCISE

- Begin with the Deep Breathing Exercise on page 165. Breathe deeply into the whole of your life. As you feel relaxed and quiet, spread the papers in front of you and label them:

  A CHILDHOOD NAME

  A NICKNAME

  A NAME OF ENDEARMENT

  A ROLE NAME (that is, a name that gave you a role, such as son, daughter, sister, brother, mother,   father, aunt, uncle, granddaughter, grandfather,   carpenter, nurse, etc.)

  MY PRESENT NAME

- Hear echoing through you the many names you have been called during your life. Choose one of the papers and write or draw that name on it. See the person that was/is yourself and answer these questions:

    Who gave me this name?

    What relationships were involved with this name?

    When I hear this name even now,

        what feelings well up inside me?

    What kind of promises was I keeping

        (or do I still keep) around this name?

    Today does anyone call me by this name?

    Do I wish someone would or could?

- Choose a second paper and answer the same questions for that name. Continue until you have completed each paper. Spread the papers once again in front of you and feel the flow of your life within your many names. Speak a quiet word of gratitude to your life for the legacy represented by your names.

FOR GROUPS:

- Get into foursomes. Take a moment for each person to select the paper with a favorite name on it. Take turns sharing whatever makes that name special to you.

vi. Beyond Bremen Town

Stories to Nurture You

EXERCISE

Five stories, pregnant with promise, encouragement, and meaning, lie open before you. The characters and metaphors in each speak to you, become you, and nurture you as you live your own story.

> THE BREMEN TOWN MUSICIANS
> Donkey, Dog, Cat, Rooster face the unknown together, and together create a future.

> A HOUSE FOR HERMIT CRAB
> Hermit Crab moves with caution and care from shell to shell, and the patterns of his life emerge with their possibilities and power.

> BIMWILI & THE ZIMWI
> Bimwili, the child, singer of her own song, at last has a story to tell and a shell to show.

> FREDERICK
> Frederick gathers at the old stone wall, opens the treasures of inner seeing in his life, and in turn receives his name.

> MISS RUMPHIUS
> Miss Rumphius unfolds her life, reveals her beauty grown out of sickness, the dark and the cold. She plants new seeds out of her "divine madness" as home becomes everywhere.

• At this period in your life, which of the five stories draws you the most? When you know, be open to that story with all your heart, mind, and body. Purchase a copy of this particular story or check it out of the library. Enjoy the drawings in the book. Keep the characters and the metaphors of this story before you. Reread the chapter in this book that relates to "your" story. Become one with the story as it becomes deeply your story also.

FOR GROUPS:

• Display all five children's stories, if possible. Take time to look at each, especially if you have not seen it before. Gather in a circle and share what the stories and this group have meant to you.

Annotated Bibliography

ike favored people and places, books have a way of
offering themselves as protective, warm shells for deep
inner work. Many books have surrounded us throughout our lives and during the writing of this book. Some
authors have woven themselves so deeply into the very
fabric of our souls that one work or two is almost impossible
to single out. Through their wonderful words, these five
writers have become intimate, unseen friends whose whole
body of writing we recommend:

May Sarton's journals are soul histories of one life's emerging wisdom, hard-won in personal and professional struggle. Especially powerful are *Journal of a Solitude* (New York:
W.W. Norton, 1973), *At Seventy* (New York, W.W. Norton,
1984), and *Endgame* (New York: W.W. Norton, 1992). Her
novels, especially *As We Are Now* (New York, W.W. Norton,
1973) and *A Reckoning* (New York, W.W. Norton, 1978),
create rich, complex worlds of passion and compassion.
Recently, it is her poetry that speaks to us with great power.

Helen M. Luke we met personally when our manuscript was
in a very rustic stage. In addition to her face-to-face and phone
guidance, her writing nourished this book and our lives. Each
sentence of her volume *Old Age: Journey into Simplicity* (New
York: Parabola Books, 1987) comes packed with insights into

the "gift of aging." This book, more than any other, helped us understand and love the transformative mysteries of old age. Also noteworthy is *Kaleidoscope* (New York: Parabola Books, 1992), her breath-taking collection of essays gathered from the last three decades of her writing.

Abraham Joshua Heschel's words, especially *I Asked for Wonder: A Spiritual Anthology* (New York: Crossroads, 1987), sustained us in the limbo between our earliest vision of this book and the very rough first drafts. The chapter "To Grow in Wisdom" from *The Insecurity of Freedom* (New York: Schocken Books, 1966) gave us courage and confirmed what we experienced in our work with older people.

Henri J. M. Nouwen writes with passion and deep spiritual insight about any topic he touches. We particularly recommend *Aging* (New York: Doubleday Image, 1974), *The Wounded Healer* (New York: Doubleday, 1979), and *Life of the Beloved: Spiritual Living in a Secular World* (New York: Crossroad, 1992).

Ira Progoff's Intensive Journal system of personal and spiritual growth has formed the core of our adult lives. If you feel journal writing may be a way of inner growth, you can find rich sources in *At a Journal Workshop* (New York: Dialogue House, 1975) and *The Practice of Process Meditation* (New York: Dialogue House, 1980). For an even deeper experience of this method, you may wish to attend a Journal Workshop in your area. For information, call Dialogue House 1-800-221-5844.

Under the general headings of AGING, PSYCHOLOGY, WOMEN'S STUDIES, and SPIRITUALITY, we have selected several books to recommend. Each of these books has had a definite, direct influence on certain sections of our own work.

AGING

When I Am An Old Woman I Shall Wear Purple, An Anthology of Short Stories and Poetry. Edited by Sandra Martz. Manhattan Beach, California: Papier-Mache, 1987.

> This collection of stories, essays, poems, and photographs is devoted to the stories of ordinary women moving into and through the aging process. It lets us know some of the unexpected rewards of aging while poignantly touching the heart.

The Courage to Grow Old. Edited by Philip L. Berman. New York: Ballantine Books, 1989.

> Gathered here are thought-provoking essays of well-known persons who reflect on their experience of old age. The spirit and energy in these pages reveals the liberation that comes with this period of life.

Chinen, Allan B. *In the Ever After: Fairy Tales and the Second Half of Life.* Wilmette, Illinois: Chiron Publications, 1989.

> This collection of Elder Tales and the commentary on each easily engages the imagination and draws the reader into the richness of the aging process. Excellent for classes in aging, as well as for individual reading.

Erikson, Erik, Joan Kivnick, and Helen Q. Erikson. *Vital Involvement in Old Age: The Experience of Old Age in Our Time.* New York: W. W. Norton & Company, 1986.

> This book fleshes out the developmental tasks of old age — balancing integrity versus despair to gain wisdom. The use of Bergman's "Wild Strawberries" demonstrates how entry into our life story keeps us vitally involved.

PSYCHOLOGY

Satir, Virginia. *Making Contact.* Millbrae, California: Celestial Arts, 1976.

> This clear and understandable guide to being in contact with the self and others is written in language steeped in meaning. It has long been a handbook for classes as well as personal life.

Reclaiming the Inner Child. Edited by Jeremiah Abrams. Los Angeles: Jeremy P. Tarcher, Inc., 1990.

> A scholarly collection of essays on the inner child by well-known authorities on the subject.

WOMEN'S STUDIES

Duerk, Judith. *Circle of Stones: Woman's Journey to Herself.* San Diego: LuraMedia, 1989.

> This is a book we circle back to often, a powerful re-envisioning of how our lives as women might be different if there had been for us, at stepping stone moments within our lives, a circle of strong, loving women to whom we could turn.

Estés, Clarissa Pinkola. *Women Who Run with the Wolves: Myths and Stories of the Wild Woman Archetype*. New York: Ballantine, 1992.

> Our first response to this massive book was to eat it in one gulp. Riveting. Un-put-downable. Then we slowed to savor each mythic and story image, knowing there is nurturance here for a lifetime. Wonderful for women to share, unfolding with each other, as a means of sharing their lifestories.

Reis, Patricia. *Through the Goddess: A Woman's Way of Healing*. New York: Continuum, 1991.

> Brilliantly researched, this book brings a visual artist's eye to the human record of spiritual searching. The author uses her extensive knowledge of the religious remains of past cultures to speak to today's woman, especially about the images of the abused body, the wounded body, and the deficient body and how these can be transformed into the celebrated, the healed, and the fulfilled body.

Anderson, Sherry R., and Patricia Hopkins. *The Feminine Face of God: The Unfolding of the Sacred in Women*. New York: Bantam Books, 1991.

> How we wish this book had been present to us in our growing up years! It chronicles the spiritual searches of women from many religious traditions who by the power and clarity of their own spirits are able to live within and beyond patriarchies in fruitful and fulfilling ways. It encompasses the essence of spirituality: women believing in their own inner truth and telling that truth in their stories.

SPIRITUALITY

In addition to the women's books mentioned above, all of which are deeply spiritual, we recommend the following books as sustenance for anyone wishing to deepen the inner journey.

Buechner, Frederick. *The Sacred Journey.* San Francisco: Harper and Row, 1982.
> The author's memoirs of his childhood are presented in profound simplicity. A readable, moving book that invites the reader to consider the sacredness in the everyday happenings within a life.

benShea, Noah. *Jacob, the Baker: Gentle Wisdom for a Complicated World.* New York: Villard Books, 1989. *Jacob's Journey: Wisdom to Find the Way, Strength to Carry On.* New York: Villard Books, 1991.
> These two books, with their simple, almost Hasidic tales, are storehouses of wisdom. Jacob's words are like yeast for a meaningful life. They never cease to calm our spirits and gently remind us of the deep truths of life.

Johnston, William. *Silent Music.* New York: Harper and Row, 1974.
> In its four major parts, "Meditation," "Consciousness," "Healing," and "Intimacy," this classic work on the meeting points of Eastern and Western mystical traditions offers a well-informed "science of meditation." Particularly notable are the lyrical sections on "Mystical Friendship" and "Friendship — the cosmic dimension."

Moore, Thomas. *Care of the Soul.* New York: Harper Collins, 1992.

> This artfully written book challenges us to live with "soul." It weaves religion, psychology, and spirituality and shows us that life is not a problem to be solved but rather an opportunity for soul making.

Houston, Jean. *The Possible Human.* Los Angeles: Jeremy Tarcher, Inc., 1982. *The Search for The Beloved.* Los Angeles, Jeremy Tarcher, Inc., 1987.

> We strongly recommend attendance at any workshop by Jean Houston, who, in her inimitable, delightful way, opens participants through stories and the arts to connect within themselves and to the universe around them. These two books are the result of her workshops and are especially good resources for groups.

Franck, Frederick. *The Zen of Seeing: Seeing/Drawing as Meditation.* New York: Vintage Books, 1973. *The Awakened Eye.* New York: Vintage Books, 1979.

> Frederick Franck's books, complete with his exquisite drawings, have a way of making everyday life feel as holy as he — and we — believe it to be. If you think drawing may offer a way of inner growth, you can find rich rewards here.

Burnham, Sophy. *A Book of Angels.* New York: Ballantine, 1990. *Angel Letters.* New York: Ballantine, 1991.

Since these beautifully documented and illustrated companion volumes found their way into our hearts, we have been unable to keep a copy on hand, so quickly do they make their way into other lives. These books are a celebration of the extraordinariness of very ordinary lives and of the closeness of loving spirits to us all.

About the Authors

Dorothy Albracht Doherty (B.A., Elem. Ed., MSW, CSW) *was born into a dairy farming family of nine in Nazareth, Texas. With this rich beginning, she became a Benedictine nun and for years taught primary grades before entering the field of social work. Since then, she has worked in England and, on returning to the States, began her work specifically teaching and counseling older students. She has a private practice, counsels in homes of the disabled elderly, conducts seminars and retreats on aging, self-esteem, widowhood, journaling, and women's issues. She lives in Chicago, Illinois, with her husband and three children.*

Mary Colgan McNamara (B.A., Eng., and Phil, M.A., Eng.) *received her love for human communities from her large family and the School Sisters of St. Francis among whom she taught and did community development in the U.S. and Latin America. Along with advanced studies in Spirituality and Women's Studies, she has custom-designed seminars on the interior life, prayer, liberation theology, music fantasy, and journal writing. She is a consultant with EXCEL, INC., giving workshops on learning styles and brain research, curriculum design, and organizational change. She lives in Tampa, Florida, with her husband, two sons, and the night music of three cats.*

Dorothy and Mary lead both separate and shared lives, yet the distance of miles has served to intensify their communication and, ultimately, the development of this book. Now in their formative years, they continue to search for "glory holes" within their lives and find intense fire in the areas of the nature of transformative memory and the creation of intentional communities of older persons. Finished neither as women nor as writers, they share their dreamings and enthusiasms in this part of their journeys out of the skin into the soul.

Other LuraMedia Publications

BANKSON, MARJORY ZOET

Braided Streams:
Esther and a Woman's Way of Growing

Seasons of Friendship:
Naomi and Ruth as a Pattern

"This Is My Body. . .":
Creativity, Clay, and Change

BOHLER, CAROLYN STAHL

Prayer on Wings: *A Search for Authentic Prayer*

**DOHERTY, DOROTHY ALBRACHT
and McNAMARA, MARY COLGAN**

Out of the Skin Into the Soul:
The Art of Aging

GEIGER, LURA JANE

***and* PATRICIA BACKMAN**

Braided Streams Leader's Guide

***and* SUSAN TOBIAS**

Seasons of Friendship Leader's Guide

GOODSON, WILLIAMSON (with Dale J.)

Re-Souled: *Parallel Spiritual Awakening of a
Psychiatrist and His Patient in Alcohol Recovery*

JEVNE, RONNA FAY

It All Begins With Hope:
Patients, Caretakers, and the Bereaved Speak Out

***and* ALEXANDER LEVITAN**

No Time for Nonsense:
Getting Well Against the Odds

KEIFFER, ANN

Gift of the Dark Angel: *A Woman's Journey
through Depression toward Wholeness*

LODER, TED

Eavesdropping on the Echoes:
Voices from the Old Testament

Guerrillas of Grace:
Prayers for the Battle

Tracks in the Straw:
Tales Spun from the Manger

Wrestling the Light:
Ache and Awe in the Human-Divine Struggle

MEYER, RICHARD C.

One Anothering:
Biblical Building Blocks for Small Groups

MILLETT, CRAIG

In God's Image:
Archetypes of Women in Scripture

PRICE, H.H.

Blackberry Season:
A Time to Mourn, A Time to Heal

RAFFA, JEAN BENEDICT

The Bridge to Wholeness:
A Feminine Alternative to the Hero Myth

SAURO, JOAN

Whole Earth Meditation:
Ecology for the Spirit

SCHAPER, DONNA

A Book of Common Power:
Narratives Against the Current

Stripping Down:
The Art of Spiritual Restoration

WEEMS, RENITA J.

Just a Sister Away: *A Womanist Vision
of Women's Relationships in the Bible*

I Asked for Intimacy: *Stories of Blessings,
Betrayals, and Birthings*

The Women's Series

BORTON, JOAN

Drawing from the Women's Well:
Reflections on the Life Passage of Menopause

CARTLEDGE-HAYES, MARY

To Love Delilah:
Claiming the Women of the Bible

DUERK, JUDITH

Circle of Stones:
Woman's Journey to Herself

I Sit Listening to the Wind:
Woman's Encounter within Herself

**O'HALLORAN, SUSAN *and*
DELATTRE, SUSAN**

The Woman Who Lost Her Heart:
A Tale of Reawakening

RUPP, JOYCE

The Star in My Heart:
Experiencing Sophia, Inner Wisdom

SCHNEIDER-AKER, KATHERINE

God's Forgotten Daughter:
*A Modern Midrash: What If
Jesus Had Been A Woman?*

the
WOMEN'S
series

LuraMedia, Inc. , 7060 Miramar Rd., Suite 104, San Diego, CA 92121
Call 1-800-FOR-LURA for information about bookstores or ordering.
Books for Healing and Hope, Balance and Justice.